FREEDOM AND COMMUNITY

FREEDOM
AND
COMMUNITY

Yves R. Simon

Edited by
Charles P. O'Donnell

Introduction by
Eugene Kennedy

Fordham University Press
New York
2001

Library of Congress Cataloging-in-Publication Data

Simon, Yves René Marie, 1903–1961.
    Freedom and community / by Yves R. Simon ; edited by
Charles P. O'Donnell; introduction by Eugene Kennedy.
      p.   cm.
    Originally published: 1968.
    Includes bibliographical references and index.
    ISBN 0-8232-2106-7 (hardcover) — ISBN 0-8232-2107-5 (pbk.)
    1. Liberty.   2. Authority.   3. Community.   I. O'Donnell,
Charles Peter, 1904– II. Title.
JC585 .S517   2001
320'.01'1—dc21   2001033283

In memory of John Courtney Murray, s.j.,
who with Yves Simon labored for freedom

Contents

Introduction

For pilgrims making their way across the burned out and burning desert of contemporary American culture the work of philosopher Yves R. Simon rises at first like a shimmering mirage, so green and welcoming, so hospitable to the weary and confused as to defy being true. So many once-promising destinations have proved to be delusions, as fragile as movie-set façades whose doors open only on the wildness beyond.

In fact, Simon's work is a true oasis whose shelter and shade are real. Yet one learns quickly that this haven, thick with date palms and clear springs, is hardly a spa in which the weary and troubled are allowed to rest as they are nourished at the feast of his thought. The condition for entry, indeed, that one essential for renewal and refreshment, is, for curious travelers, hard work, including a readiness to think through with a master teacher the fundamental concepts of life that they may think they already comprehend. For Americans, these include terms polished so smooth by the advertising and public relations complex—notions of freedom, liberty, authority, and the common good—that their surfaces gleam, masking their emptiness and making them appear nourishing when they are not.

Readers should not proceed further, then, if they are unprepared to read and think and read again about concepts that are in such common play that many believe that a common understanding of their meaning also exists. The oasis of Simon's work blooms, however, when we understand, as he points out in many ways, that philosophy, like virtue, is pursued, not merely by the curious intellect, but also by the person totally engaged—imagination, heart, and soul—in the process. Readers will not rest but they will be refreshed as, against the grain of the pragmatism and utilitarianism that sheathe and soothe American life, they accept this challenge.

First Truth, Hard Truth

This necessary commitment of the inquiring person is, in fact, the theme of the first chapter, "Freedom in Daily Life," written by Simon shortly after the Second World War, as he viewed the wreckage, not only of Europe's cities, but also of the pre-war liberal beliefs that were ruinously tested by totalitarian propaganda. The disaster suffered by so many ordinary people was a function of their buying in at such a steep price to the policies of their less than common leaders who felt that, yes, one could live well enough without true freedom. Their horrendous political decisions had not arisen from their full-hearted longing for peace, as much an illusion as the concrete trench of their Maginot Line, but from their failure to quarry out within themselves the conviction that freedom cannot live without truth.

They thus seasoned with sand the foundation for moral choice and the common good that soon collapsed. Propaganda, as Simon reflects later, triumphs readily when people are unwilling to do the hard work of facing what we might, in our own time, call the first and hardest of truths: either freedom and truth cohere or they disintegrate rapidly into slogans.

As he left the presidency, Dwight D. Eisenhower warned the United States against the "Military/Industrial Complex" that he felt might transform and come to dominate American culture. A more insidious enemy, however, has been the Advertising/

Public Relations Complex, recognized long before by Simon as the propaganda engines of coercion, that have emptied the great concepts of democracy of their gravity and transformed them into weightless phrases and brand names, easily marketed for the political wars. Freedom has lost the robust dimensions that, almost alone of the philosophers of our time, Simon explores in rich and compelling detail. It has become identified with individual choice, a concept that was first beggared and then promoted as the highest defining right of all Americans. Choice, in and of itself, shorn of object, circumstances, or consequences, has been glorified as the American way in everything, from choosing a faith to selecting a car, from aborting new life to terminating old ones.

As Peter Drucker has written of American choices, you can either work or go to meetings but you cannot do both, so Yves Simon reminds us that the weightier elements of our choices—those so startling that, were they to be proclaimed by a public figure, they would cause a panic—freedom, including that of choice, and truth, its code and context, cannot survive without each other.

Thus, in these pages, and in his other books, manuscripts, and even in the class notes of his students, Simon anticipates the epistemological crisis of our time in which a soft totalitarianism so confounds truth and illusion, fact and appearance, camouflage and reality, that the losses we thereby suffer are never calculated. We accept instead the almost comfortable exile, as in a low security ungated prison or a high security gated community, from doing the hard work of being moral persons with obligations to the truth we must fulfill for our own sake and for the common good. This American dream of the good life is achieved by self-serving economic activity. The humanly good life, however, is attained only by self-sacrificing moral activity.

Simon understands and repeatedly stresses that the virtuous life is located in the soul and heart and that reflections and celebrations of this must excite the imagination rather than just the will. This applies to religion as well. He centers us in the human person; prodding us to understand that all the speaking parts, as distinguished from the faceless crowd extras, demand that we write our own lines rather than read dialogue prepared by another. Beyond that, all transforming and enriching activity, including citizenship in a democracy, demands that we speak these lines from within ourselves and thereby enrich and strengthen not only ourselves but also the community of which we are members.

Simon identifies our human moral action, therefore, not as reciting somebody else's lines, but as searching ever more deeply for the words that capture the truth about our experience together and in community. Being human and exercising our liberty is *dynamic* rather than static, active rather than passive, an overflow of the imagination rather than a flexing of the will. In a grief-plagued time, people have come to accept Sigmund Freud's insight that mourning is not something that can be papered over with activity, or denied. It is a human activity that finally demands that, on every level of our being, we take it up as *work to be done* that cannot be done for us by another. Simon makes us aware that the life of the moral person or the good citizen makes the same demand on every level of our personalities. It is work that engages our whole selves and it cannot be delegated to others. We carry it out by and for ourselves or we fail and its fruits never ripen within us or within our communities. As we build our own moral character so, too, we enlarge the common good.

Authority

Hannah Arendt has written that our contemporary moral plight is related to our "not understanding what authority is." Yves Simon does understand authority and invites us all to think freshly about this gravely misunderstood but essential element. Indeed, it is difficult to appreciate contemporary problems without a clear understanding that their common denominator is a distortion, or total negation, of the idea of authority. It is no accident that authority and its proper exercise became a sub-text of the 2000 American presidential election for, as one aide to former President Clinton expressed it, they "did not value structure enough." In other words, they had no clear idea of the importance of authority. Americans revel in what they construe to be freedom, although, as Simon notes, they miss its grandeur by reducing liberty to total immunity from coercion or to the ability to do whatever they want, to be free, as atoms are alleged to be by physicists, of any determination.

Authority is chronically confused with authoritarianism, the rigid coercion of others by instruments of power, not the least of which, as Simon observes, is the propaganda that is now the product of the Advertising/Public Relations Complex. Paradoxically, Americans are enchanted with power and, indeed, describe a democratic triumph for the individual as empowerment. Yet, as any reader of Simon learns, power is to authority as lust is to love, that is to say, an incendiary and manipulative assault on the fullness of human activity in legislation or in love.

Authority may be understood, then, as a dynamic human activity. Its root is the Latin *augere*, meaning "to grow," "to increase," "to create." Here is the vocabulary for Simon's understanding of authority as a necessary human activity that is essential for the autonomy of the individual and the flourishing of the common good. Other concepts from the same root include "author" and "augment." They share the connotation of healthy growth, of bringing something new into being. For Simon, authority is not a negative abstract that suppresses human freedom and development. Quite the contrary.

One exercises authority *dynamically*, that is, in and through the total involvement of the personality in relationship to another personality. Authority is aimed not at the isolated will to make it conform but rather at the integrating imagination to help it bear fruit. Education comes from *e-ducere*, "to draw out," a perfect fit with dynamic authority whether it is exercised by the schoolmaster from his podium, the preacher from his pulpit, or the president from the oval office. The task in a democracy in which Simon's understanding of the profound relationship of liberty and authority is realized is not to coerce the person or the masses to bland unanimity, but to free their growth from within. The chief authority does make an existential and influential moral difference if he lives morally and truthfully.

What happens when someone exercises authority in healthy dynamic fashion? That is, when the authority, be it parent or professor, relates to a separate person, child or student, in a dynamic human fashion that allows that person to develop, to become, as a result, someone different, someone richer, greater, more himself or herself. Healthy authority helps the individual to grow and the community to flourish at the same time. The late symphony conductor Sir Georg Solti once said that he directed so that the musicians would surpass themselves in their playing.

This is a far cry from the populist political wars in which men and women are propagandized to become less themselves and think and act less for themselves than to become members of a class, as in a class action suit, to be set aggressively against some other group. The latter despoils the virtues necessary for a democracy, setting class against class, dissolving any concept of a common good and weakening and softening every layer that it must keep under control in order to allow its few powerful leaders to survive.

The unidentified tragedy of a culture that is dominated by the techniques and unique characteristics, such as normless ethics of the Advertising/Public Relations Complex, is that the personal growth of its citizens is so stunted that, like those who die in infancy, they never develop their true gifts or become themselves. Not only are they denied full personal citizenship but, as Simon notes, this "lack of personal development jeopardizes the autonomy of the group as well as the person." And, as he also understands, true liberty, rather than a lack of coercion or determination, is "needed for bringing up people motivated for love." So, too, this liberty is "necessary on account of the nature of moral progress."

Yves Simon died in 1961, a witness to the consequences of

the Faustian pact that world leaders had made when they confounded truth and freedom, selling them out, one for the other at perilous discount. It is remarkable that his keen powers of observation allowed him to see to the very end, and beyond, of the twentieth century. Reading him, one feels in the company of an unhurried and infinitely patient traveler who understands that, although we may think we have searched for cool green relief in the desert we view from the train window, we must look at it many times, examining it from different angles, if we are to understand the mystery beneath its familiarity, and find, as he has, the sweet secret streams that carry wisdom as well as water.

The vast expanse, he understands, is ancient, its crystal sands enriched by the bones of those long lost from memory. Know them each and know them all and you will return to the same questions that he examines with a depth and discipline that surprise, stir, and refresh us even now. What Yves Simon teaches, in his gentle but exhilarating way, is that we must draw something deep from inside ourselves, deep as the wells we must find, as he did, in what can seem the trackless wastes of our culture. Our human calling is to make them bloom. This is not easy, he reminds us, but it is necessary. He offers us a way to look at ourselves so that we can see what is before out eyes. That is what a true authority does and what, perhaps later, perhaps sooner, you will understand that Yves Simon does still.

December 22, 2000 EUGENE KENNEDY

Acknowledgments

Professor Simon's reputation as a political philosopher has been so closely associated with the idea of authority that his dedication to freedom and his philosophy of freedom might have been obscured. I am therefore particularly gratified that Mrs. Paule Simon graciously invited me to examine her husband's papers on freedom and to prepare a book which would turn up the freedom side of the political coin.

Chapters I and VI in this volume were originally published by Henry Holt in 1947 in a book entitled *Community of the Free*, now out of print. Mrs. Simon, who holds the copyright on this material, has granted permission to reprint it. I am grateful to the American Catholic Philosophical Association for permission to use Professor Simon's article (Chapter II) on "Liberty and Authority" which appeared in the *Proceedings* of the Association in 1940. Chapters III, IV and V of this volume consist of Professor Simon's essays on "Freedom and Community" and on "Political Society" originally prepared for classes taught at the University of Chicago in the spring of 1955. It is our good fortune that Professor Vukan Kuic, now of the University of South Carolina, kept excellent notes on these lectures. Professor Kuic kindly consented to allow me to use his notes. Passages from them have been incorporated into the text and are identified where appropriate.

In the preparation of this book particular thanks are owed to Dr. Riley Hughes, the Georgetown University Editor, and to Robin Friedheim, the Assistant Editor. I also wish to thank the several persons who read portions of the text and kindly gave me their comments on it. I owe special thanks to Mrs. Mary Abbie Sturgeon for all of her assistance in preparing the manuscript. The Index was prepared by Rev. Dominic Hughes, O.P.

Chapters I, II, and VI are virtually identical with the printed texts. The materials of Chapters III, IV, and V were originally intended by Professor Simon for publication in his proposed "Philosophical Encyclopedia." This work remained incomplete at his untimely death in 1961. The manuscript from which these chapters have been taken contains a number of asides, incomplete references, and ideas marked for further development. In editing this text it has been my purpose to remain faithful to the language and the thought of Professor Simon and at the same time to produce a complete and integrated book.

I am under heavy obligations to Professor Kuic. He agreed to comment on the draft of Chapters III, IV, and V. His excellent suggestions and observations made it possible to improve on the presentation of these most important chapters.

Mrs. Paule Simon and her son, Anthony Simon, greatly assisted me in preparing this volume.

In editing this volume the following works have been consulted: John A. Lucal, S.J., "Yves R. Simon's Theory of Authority," master's thesis, Loyola University, Chicago, Illinois, 1963; Rev. Gerald Gehringer, "The Concept of Political Liberty according to Mortimer Adler and Yves Simon," thesis, Pontificia Universitas Lateranensis, Facultas Philosophiae, Roma, 1962.

Charles P. O'Donnell

Editor's Preface

I first met Professor Simon shortly after he arrived in the United States from France, just before World War II, at the invitation of the University of Notre Dame. During those years we had many conversations about politics and philosophy. The democratic spirit, which is so marked in his writings, exhibited itself everywhere in these conversations. I remember particularly with what pride he spoke of his grandfather's participation in a demonstration against Napoleon III.

In 1940, speaking at Marquette University on the "Nature and Functions of Authority," Professor Simon set for himself the task of discovering the principles relating to freedom and authority. He later pursued this subject in a magisterial volume published by the University of Chicago Press as *Philosophy of Democratic Government*, in 1951. By this time he was at the University of Chicago as a member of the Committee on Social Thought, under the chairmanship of Professor John U. Nef. Before Professor Simon died in 1961 he had completed a further study of authority and freedom, which was published posthumously under the title *A General Theory of Authority* (University of Notre Dame Press, 1962). In each of these volumes the emphasis was on the nature, origins, and characteristics of authority and its relationship to freedom. In the essays contained in the present volume it is freedom and its bearing on authority which are stressed.

In these writings Professor Simon's thinking was greatly influenced by his personal reactions to events in Europe during the 1920s and 30s. While still in France he was disturbed by the ineptitude and feebleness of democratic government in that country after World War I. He believed that French parliamentary politicians and the intellectuals of that age, wedded to the theory and practice of outworn notions borrowed from *laissez-faire* liberalism, produced a political situation not far from anarchy. Viewing the events of the Italian war in Ethiopia, he was appalled at the indifference of European politicians to the fate of that African country and to the violation of rational moral standards in the conduct of international relations. He deplored the decline of the League of Nations portended by the Ethiopian affair in his book *La Campagne d'Ethiopie et la pensée politique Française* (Paris: Desclée, 1936). After he came to the United States, he was deeply pained by the happenings in Nazi-occupied France. To encourage his friends there, he wrote two books in French subsequently translated into English under the titles *The Road to Vichy* (New York: Sheed and Ward, 1942) and *The March to Liberation* (Milwaukee: Tower Press, 1942).

In the debate on democracy which has been going on since the 18th century no one has stated the fundamental political issue of freedom and authority more dramatically than Jean-Jacques Rousseau in the *Social Contract*: "Man is born free and everywhere is in chains. . . . What can make it legitimate?" For Professor Simon, Rousseau posed a good question but gave a bad answer. European experience before and during World War II, Professor Simon believed, gave ample proof of the bankruptcy of the Rousseauian type of liberalism.

Professor Simon set himself the task of finding a more solid philosophical basis for authority and freedom and for a theory of democracy which comports with the world we live in and can stand the test of time. In this search he sought to establish the authenticity of authority as a safeguard to freedom. In the opening sentences of his lectures on the *Nature and Functions of Authority* (Milwaukee: Marquette University Press, 1940) he said: "Both unrestricted liberty and boundless authority are fictitious concepts. Each of them implies its own negation together with the annihilation of society. . . . The essential question for every social group is that of combining rightly the forces of authority and liberty."

A. Robert Caponigri in his preface to Professor Simon's work on *A General Theory of Authority* writes that as we "seek out the basic source of Professor Yves Simon's concern with the problem of authority" the answer is that "he is fascinated by authority precisely because he is so intensely devoted to freedom, to liberty." Caponigri rightly sees Simon's passionate attachment to freedom as integral to his cultural inheritance as a Frenchman. "Simon's attachment to liberty, equality and fraternity," he further remarks, "was deepened rather than lessened by the fact that he could not accept the theoretical basis on which these ideas had been affirmed in the revolutionary context."

Professor Simon undertook the study of the philosophical roots of freedom in a volume entitled *Traité du libre arbitre* (Liège, 1951). This work, to be published in English, is a study of free choice; it examines among other things man's awareness of freedom, the relationship of freedom to judgment, and the law and liberty. It is therefore a companion piece to the essays contained in this volume, which are principally concerned with freedom as it relates to social and political philosophy.

The essays on freedom and community in the present volume enlarge on some of the theses presented in *Philosophy of Democratic Government*. They also summarize Simon's philosophical position with regard to the nature of freedom and relate his views on freedom to the events of the postwar world in which we live. These essays, written over a period of about fifteen years, illustrate the author's practical philosophical temper; his keen awareness of the events of his times; his deep concern to reach an honest appraisal of the realities which lay behind them, and the philosophical insight which enabled him to see reality as a whole without losing a grasp on its fragmented parts. It was his constant striving to understand the meaning of freedom and of authority in the affairs of practical life that led him to the explanations he presents in these essays.

The first essay in this volume, "Freedom in Daily Life," is from the volume *Community of the Free* (New York: Holt, 1947), now out of print. In this essay Professor Simon, addressing himself to the pre-World War II dilemmas of European liberal faith, reflects on the reasons why ordinary people taken in by Nazi propaganda thought they could live well without freedom. He calls our attention to the unwillingness of these ordinary persons to face up to the hard truths of life. Because they were misled by liberal indifference to the truth, they failed to understand that freedom and truth are inseparable, and they did not see through the propaganda of Fascist regimes.

In the second essay on "Liberty and Authority," written for the Catholic Philosophical Association in 1940, Yves Simon sought to disengage the idea of freedom from its concrete and existential forms. He notes that freedom takes place in deliberate actions rather than by chance. Freedom is experienced when we feel we dominate a situation. Freedom, he therefore concludes, means mastery. In my judgment Professor Simon developed a theory of freedom which Walter Lippmann in his *Preface to Morals* tried to evoke in his concept of "maturity," but with less success. Furthermore, in the course of this analysis Professor Simon anticipated the critique of communism presented in Milovan Djilas' famous volume on *The New Class*. Simon said in this essay, as Djilas later did, that totalitarianism has separated authority from its essential functions by substituting the private interest of a group of self-anointed leaders (the new class) for the common good of society as the main subject of politics.

The next three essays in this volume are taken from the manuscripts of Professor Simon on "Freedom and Community" and "Political Society." The emphasis of Simon in the first of these essays is on the significance of freedom in societies other than that of the state. Professor Simon is here concerned with freedom in terms of its deprivation. He speaks of the denial of freedom as a form of alienation such as is found in the institution of slavery and other kinds of servitude, including the alienation of men with respect to their property and work. Man as a worker, he says, is free so long as his work is employed in the common interest, and his compensation is equitable. Thus freedom in society is essential to political freedoms.

In the essay on "Political Society" Professor Simon notes the great temptation of the state to glorify itself in order to establish an imperial rule over its subject. As President John Adams once said, "Power always thinks it has a great soul." Professor Simon examines physical and psychic coercion in the state and he identifies them as instruments which, when rationally used by those in authority for the common good, can serve as pedagogues of freedom.

Many disciples of the enlightenment regarded themselves as the sole guardians of freedom. In its 18th- and 19th-century European versions, liberalism was associated with an optimistic philosophy of inevitable progress. The totalitarian doctrines of the 1920s and 1930s not only cast doubt on the inevitability of progress as an historical phenomenon but also challenged the fundamental notions of freedom and progress themselves. In the sixth essay in this volume, "Pessimism and the Philosophy of Progress," which originally appeared in *Community of the Free,* Professor Simon comments that in spite of the setbacks of the totalitarian challenge, the tremendous postwar forward surge of science and technology has created a new kind of optimism concerning material progress, but unhappily it, too, is associated with increasing doubts that man will be able to manage his own creations. "The mastery of man over human acts as distinguished from techniques can be asserted," Professor Simon maintains, "only through the knowledge of liberty and through the operations of liberty. A philosophy of progress which is wholly dependent upon technological change and technical education creates a universe of freedom, which, when totally absorbed in the universe of nature, loses its freedom."

Professor Simon proposes a theory of progress and technological change consonant with freedom which he calls an authentically pessimistic view. It is a view which perceives that "justice is not entirely absent from temporal history despite the wounds of sin. The struggle for justice is not doomed to certain failure. . . . : it is only extremely difficult. . . . True pessimism restores confidence and frees energies."

The theory of liberty propounded by Professor Simon, along with his analyses of authority, democracy, and practical wisdom, contains the elements of a political philosophy which can provide direction to other contemporary political theorists and above all to the political scientists of our times. The latter have gathered and organized great masses of political facts but lack a normative set of ideas which can make these facts meaningful and useful to political society. Professor Simon's realistic normative thinking deserves the increased attention of political scientists.

The position of Professor Simon, who is a philosopher rather than a political scientist, is that while there is a science of social and political facts, a normative moral philosophy which knows the ends of human action is necessary because men make good or bad use of their freedom. The acknowledgment of the distinction between political theory and political science and the growing recognition of the need for their reconciliation encourages one to think that political scientists may at some future time turn to political philosophers such as Simon. They will not and should not expect to find extended analyses of political facts. Such studies are not the business of a philosopher. An examination of Simon's own workmanlike study of the Ethiopian war and similar analyses of other contemporary issues should make political scientists more willing to see that philosophers like Simon not only appreciate the value of empirical studies but also know how to relate values and purposes to social facts.

The political philosophy of Yves Simon was not limited to his endeavors to restate the meaning of freedom and authority. He saw that philosophy about the world of action as a search which would take him down many parallel and crisscrossing roads. He saw, for example, that freedom and authority must be related to man's search for truth and the common good and to a practical wisdom which reconciles truth and goodness, thought, and action. Professor Simon was also always aware that his personal search was part of a joint venture. He had a profound sense of community; of the responsibility laid on individuals in society to use their talents so that the genius of the philosopher and the need for practical wisdom would not be lost, forgotten, or allowed to decay.

The 1960s, which began in the United States with the fresh and youthful promises of John F. Kennedy, have rapidly become a decade of raging doubts not only in the field of politics, but more alarmingly in philosophy itself. One sees that philosophers of all ages have differed one from the other. It is the distinction of this decade that philosophy itself is in doubt. Philosophers have become more selfconscious and more prone to air their views on all subjects philosophical and otherwise; for the time being they find themselves almost despairing of communicating with one another or with anyone else.

In years to come, philosophers, and especially political philosophers, should be able to repair to more solid ground. I believe that they will find Professor Simon has constructed a pattern of philosophical themes which will satisfy reasonable and moderate men looking for a way out of scepticism and uncertainty. Professor Simon was not a dogmatist, but he knew what he knew and what he did not know. This is the beginning of wisdom and a model for philosophers.

Among Christian critics of Thomism, uncertainty, stopping just short of radical doubt, has resulted in a search for an alternative philosophy. This effort has forced some thinkers into an uneasy reliance on religious faith as the foundation of thought and action. I believe that much of the doubt among some contemporary philosophically minded Christians is attributable to their penchant for social action. They are reaching for a philosophy which will answer their hesitations about what they should do personally in the face of contemporary concerns over sex, marriage, divorce, contraception, and the like, as well as what they should think about social, political, and cultural questions.

Yves Simon was keenly aware that the practical sciences of morals and politics, for example, are incapable of the precision of theoretical knowledge because the former includes "habits, skills which can be acquired and lost," because groups and institutions affect the realization of political action and the practicality of moral purposes, and because man lives and acts in a changing social-biological milieu. Professor Simon's effort to distinguish the essential elements of morals and politics was in part motivated by a great desire to establish rational norms in the light of which man's action in society can be judged and redressed.

The beleaguered Christian thinkers have not understood the meaning of truth in Thomistic thought. Jacques Maritain in *Le Paysan de la Garonne* (Paris: Desclée, 1966), pp. 143–44, reminds his fellow thinkers that "man has the capacity to attain truth by his own power" but that men "stumble and zigzag" on the road to truth. Maritain holds, as did Simon, that "a philosophical doctrine essentially founded on truth is at least *possible*." Its possibility, he goes on to say, depends on the work of many thinkers pursuing a common line of thought for a very long time. Such a doctrine, he remarks, "cannot be or even pretend to be, a perfect doctrine that can answer all the questions that arise in the course of time." A true doctrine, Maritain concludes, "is never finished and always progresses." This is not the language or the conviction of absolutism.

The wider acceptance of Professor Simon's theory of democracy, authority, and freedom, will not come easily. There is a strong contemporary reaction against Thomistic thought, especially among Christian thinkers, because of its alleged overemphasis on Hellenistic styles of philosophizing. Professor Simon, in a modern vein and using common-sense examples to illustrate the problems he propounds, employs a vocabulary (in this respect he is very often contemporary) which takes some time and effort to relate to his line of argument. While he has explored the ideas of freedom and authority more adequately from a philosophical point of view than almost any of his contemporaries, he did not complete the analyses he began. I am struck by the weight of his argument with regard to the pedagogical uses of coercive authority but I feel that the subject needs amplification, in part because it relates so intimately to complex and concrete situations. His critique of European liberalism needs to be amplified by further studies of British and American liberal thought in the light of the principles of freedom and authority that he has given us. I am convinced that when political theorists in the United States become more persuaded than they are today of the merits of a realistic approach to the problems of rationality and freedom in politics, Professor Simon's contribution to the advancement of this kind of thinking will be very great indeed.

We think of our times as the age of "freedom." A spirit of rebellion and a wild reaching out for ideas, and experiences denied or alleged to have been denied by the heavy hand of the past, are equated with the freedom of our times and with new insights. Crises in domestic affairs, in international relations, and in religious life and thought point to a frantic search for freedom. All are crises of freedom.

Sometime in the future there will be a stock-taking and a re-examination of the spirit of the times. The principal line of inquiry will be into the meaning of freedom in its every aspect as we prize highly what we do not have. We have yet to discover that what we have is not what we thought we had. But man will eventually endeavor to find the true meaning of freedom and seek to develop it anew.

Professor Simon's contribution to future stock-taking can be enormous. The rigor of his thought, the clarity with which he defines hard-core problems; his no-nonsense view of reality, and his non-sentimentalist love of truth and goodness will help all of those persuaded that the road to freedom needs wise and good guides. Behind Marshall McLuhan's aphorism "the medium is the message" there is the deeper truth that freedom is both the medium and the message. It is a freedom which takes hold of each person, sets him free, and perfects society. It is this concept of freedom and its uses that Professor Simon has given us.

CHARLES P. O'DONNELL

Georgetown University
Washington, D.C.

FREEDOM AND COMMUNITY

1

Freedom in Daily Life

WHEN I WAS A YOUNG STUDENT IN PARIS some twenty years
ago,* the doctrines, whether false or true, which had shaped
the course of the French nation for more than a century were
breaking up. Liberalism was the object of a rapidly spreading scorn. That the decay of liberalism should have brought
in its train the decay of the idea of freedom is nowise surprising. The whole of liberal thought in the nineteenth century
had unremittingly labored to create an indissoluble union
between a divine perfection, freedom, and a false philosophy,
liberalism. To accept in all its confusion the bond created by
liberal philosophy, and to blaspheme the divine name at the
same time that one condemned the false philosophy, was
the easiest course to pursue, the course which demanded the

* Written at the end of World War II, this chapter refers in
several places to events which occurred in Europe and elsewhere
before that war. It reproduces Chapter I of the same title of *Community of the Free* (New York: Holt, 1947), pp. 1–34.

least mental effort and the least courage. The unpardonable sin of our intellectuals is to have chosen, in that decisive moment, the road of minimum effort and minimum generosity.

Perhaps we should not so willingly have listened to the doctrinaires who, in their arrogant criticism, confounded liberalism and freedom, had we not in the back of our minds cherished an optimistic illusion which, all unconsciously, we had received from that very liberalism: the illusion that the indispensable liberties would never be seriously jeopardized in our civilized societies. The history of Hitler's Germany has rid us of that illusion. The worthiest citizens in jail, and criminals in power; the innocent, by hundreds of thousands, deprived of freedom to remain in their own homes and forced to stand in line before firing squads; the members of the accursed races driven out of economic life, then subjected to forced labor, finally massacred; the silence of truth, the dictatorship of liars—we know now that such things can take place in countries whose culture is ancient and subtle. We have come to understand that no posture of affairs, no constitution, no culture, suffices to guarantee fundamental liberties; and that nothing can protect a people from the worst forms of tyranny when a taste for an easy life and a tendency to let things take their course carry the day over a conscious, tense, and—if need be—heroic will to be free.

Today we frequently hear it remarked that the privilege of freedom has to be rewon once in every generation—or, say, three or four times a century. Even that is too much optimism. Freedom is impregnably assured only by an effort to conquer it which is renewed every day. In the course of the great series of catastrophes which resulted in the re-enslavement of peoples who had been amongst the first to shatter the ancient despotisms, we had numerous opportunities to observe the functioning of the secret complicities which made victory for the enslavers possible and inevitable. All around us, mingled with us in our daily life, people reputedly honorable showed by their words, their attitudes, their silences, their resignations, that they had not the souls of free men. In these cases it was not a question of a philosophic attitude, as it was in the case of the intellectuals just mentioned; only a moral attitude was involved. More or less consciously, but always with a terrible consistency, these people gave the enemy the most precious of all information —the revelation of their indifference, not to say their hostility, towards that which the enslavers wished to destroy. They did not want freedom for others; nor did they want it for themselves. They wanted money, security, consideration, power, and also the cherished satisfactions of arrogance and vengeance. They believed, fundamentally, that one can live very well without freedom. One can also live without dignity, if one has a liking for baseness. As St. Bernard has it, freedom and dignity are one. *Dignitatem in homine liberum arbitrium voco.* There, precisely, is the thing in which the enslavers are interested, and more especially those consummate masters of enslavement, the Nazis. As material for their enterprises, they must have men who have lost their self-respect.

The Spirit of Freedom and the Spirit of Truth

In observing those anonymous accomplices of tyranny, those ordinary people, those honorable people, those decent people who had never committed murder or stolen, but who did not have the souls of free men, we were often struck by one paradoxical characteristic: a systematic hatred of truth. Not only did they delight in falsehoods which flattered their passions, they also reached the point of preferring falsehoods in trivial matters. It sometimes seemed that, if the choice were to be made, they would have preferred an unpleasant falsehood to an agreeable truth. Their entire behavior suggested that the poor devils were well aware that opening the door to truth is a rather disquieting operation; that once truth is brought into our dwellings, she is likely to conduct us where we do not want to go; that if we let truth take possession of our minds, we run the risk of having her drag us out of our decadence and carry us towards a destiny not of comfort but of greatness.

Between the spirit of truth and the spirit of freedom there is a relation to which liberalism has made us insensitive.[1] Yet it is a relation declared by the Gospels. It is a perfectly intelligible relation. Freedom is the power to make a choice between the means offered to our activity. Now, there are authentic means, those which lead to the end, and illusory means, those which lead us away from our end. Freedom to choose illusory means is itself only an illusion of freedom, for a means which does not lead to the end is not a means. But how should my will be protected against the fearsome possibility of choosing illusory means, of making wrong choices, if my intellect is in error? All of our real freedom is contained within the limits of our knowledge of truth. Outside of those limits, in the field of error, there is room for no operation but the disastrous one of choosing a means which is not a means. *And ye shall know the truth, and the truth shall make you free* (John 8, 32). The spirit of freedom has no worse enemy than falsehood. The conquest of freedom in daily life implies above all else a daily fight against falsehood, a daily fight for truth.

[1] We do not refer here to any particular doctrine in politics or economics, but to the general attitude of liberalism with regard to the problem of truth. The theories held by liberal movements concerning freedom of the mind often convey the idea that freedom has no meaning if there is such a thing as absolute truth and suggest that some amount of indifferentism is an indispensable condition for the preservation of freedom in society.

We shall have not the slightest chance of fighting this fight successfully so long as we have not comprehended what a difficult fight it is. It is comfortable to believe what is affirmed around us, what is currently said in our family circle, amongst our friends, amongst our companions at work and in our leisure hours; what is printed in the newspapers which respectable people like ourselves are in the habit of reading; what is officially declared by the social authorities who are as it were the conscience of our group. Yet it can occur that the milieu in which we live is given over to the powers of falsehood. It occurs very often. To a certain extent, it always occurs, for there is no human society (I say, no *purely human* society), however restricted and privileged one may suppose it to be, which is devoted to truth totally and with no admixture whatever.

But let us keep in mind the present situation of the societies in which we live. I do not know, I cannot imagine, any group which does not include amongst its current ideas an enormous dose of lies. That being the case, the alternative is inevitable: either one must like falsehood, or one must dislike the familiar setting of daily life. Let us understand that it is hardly possible to ask of a man a harder sacrifice than this: for love of truth, he be ready to say No to what is thought and said every day by "his brothers and his fellows"; ready to discover the ravages of falsehood in the souls of those who are dear to him, and to continue to cherish their souls whilst he hates their lies; ready ceaselessly to unveil the lies of his own conscience. Negation and revolt are attitudes which have a certain charm, provided that the attitude which I reject and against which I revolt is voiced at a comfortable distance from my own person. But if I adopt the attitude of saying No to all falsehoods, including those which are manufactured and propagated around me as well as those which I feel welling up in myself, I know that I am setting out into a fearsome solitude, into a desert country, without roads and without water. There my dearest companions will fail me. My habits, my tastes, my passions will abandon me. With no support but truth, I shall go forward, stripped and trembling.

One thinks twice before making such a decision. Furthermore, it is a decision that will never be made once and for all, because the seductions of falsehood will never disarm. It will have to be repeated, all the ruptures that it implies will have to be accepted over again, each time that the wish for an easy life makes itself heard. Reflecting upon this program for life, we feel ourselves overwhelmed with agony. The real problem is now propounded: we must learn whether we love truth so much that we are willing to live with it, if need be, in agony, or whether we wish to avoid agony at all costs, even at the cost of truth.

The Truth about Timely Issues

This daily vigilance of the spirit of truth is above all to be exercised in one's reading of newspapers. Everyone is agreed that the press propagates a great many errors. But it is generally assumed that if I accept and propagate the error published by the newspaper to which I subscribe, the responsibility rests wholly upon the reporter, the director, the editorial board, the clique or the party which finances the newspaper, and not at all upon myself, the ordinary reader, who am obliged to put my confidence in what the printed page presents to me. There is something odiously pharisaical in such protestations of innocence on the part of the newspaper reader. Does our duty to defend our intellect from falsehood cease when a falsehood is printed on cheap paper? On the other hand, it is generally considered that newspapers are divided into two classes: the good ones, which deserve entire confidence, and the bad ones, which deserve none whatever. But what is the criterion of the good newspaper? It is here that the shoe pinches.

What is called a "good" newspaper is one which never mentions religion except in respectful terms, which does not publish obscene stories, and which expresses itself tactfully in matters of morals. Thus, four commandments are obeyed. Obviously this is better than if all ten commandments were broken. But, after all, it is not for us to make cuts in the tables of the law. I cannot call that paper a good paper which indulges in insults, incites to hatred, and breaks the fifth commandment. I cannot call that paper a good paper which indulges in defamation, and breaks the fifth, seventh, eighth, and tenth commandments. I cannot call that paper a good paper which lies. But if we include the Ten Commandments in the criterion of the good newspaper, there are very few good newspapers left.

Let us take it for granted that I have little likelihood of being able to find, for my daily information, a newspaper so good that it deserves to be taken at its word. Once I have understood this, I feel tempted to abstain. I shall read the papers in order to do what everyone else does, in order that I may be able to follow a conversation. But I shall suspend judgment. And if I am asked my opinion upon a question of the day, I shall answer that, being without a positive knowledge of the truth in the matter—or, as many people put it, being without a knowledge of the whole truth—I believe it my duty to say nothing and to think nothing.

If this attitude could be practiced consistently and sincerely, it would still be reprehensible. It often occurs that the justice of a cause requires the mobilization of all right-thinking men: to suspend judgment, to abstain, is, under such circumstances, to desert. But the attitude cannot be put into practice consistently, and the inconsistency of those who claim to have adopted it testifies to their lack of sincerity. They suspend judgment with a great show of virtue when they fear the truth: it is then that they declare (and at no great cost to themselves) that they will wait until they know the whole truth before passing judgment. The next instant they unhesitatingly pass judgment upon some other question. They are just as far from knowing the whole truth as they were in the previous instance; but they know that they are in a position to get a hearing for some proposition which makes for the side they have chosen. They look with suspicion on a certain source of information when the information supplied puts them in the wrong; they cite the same source with assurance when it puts them in the right. We shall find ourselves compelled to imitate these hypocrites every time that we undertake to practice a systematic abstention in respect to events which demand a taking of sides. The force of social life will wrench us out of our abstentions. But our taking of sides will then be disorderly and dishonest.

Actually it is not very difficult to distinguish between those events in respect to which I have a right—or perhaps even a duty—to remain with no settled opinion, and those which lay me under an obligation to pronounce judgment. Propaganda (in many of its aspects a thing so harmful) has this to be said for it—that it makes the ordinary decent citizen realize what a value interested parties set upon his opinion. Every time that an event becomes the object of assiduous propaganda intended to make me accept a certain interpretation of it, I am clearly warned that the reactions of public opinion in regard to that event stand a strong chance of furthering either justice or injustice. Accordingly, it is my duty to do all that I can to put the force of my opinion at the service of justice. When propaganda of a vehemence heretofore unknown attempted to convince world opinion that the war waged by Italy in Ethiopia was thoroughly justified, as an enterprise whose success was of vital interest to the safety of civilization; when rival propagandas wished to force upon us contradictory versions of the war in Spain and of its principal episodes; when propaganda directed with extraordinary skill described the Czechoslovakian state as a historic monstrosity, the product of perverse imaginations and diabolical designs; when untiring campaigns presented the persecution of the Jews as a mere measure of legitimate defense against intolerable abuses—honest men understood that abstention was unallowable: to abstain was to run too great a risk of serving crime. An honest man could not permit himself to take such a risk.

A firm resolve to seek out the truth in spite of propaganda and conventions is, in many cases, enough to dissipate confusion. This resolve once generously made, we become aware that the difficulties of the task are not as peculiar to itself as we had at first supposed. We encounter similar difficulties in private life, and do not consider them above our strength. Many journalists deceive themselves and seek to deceive us. But in our relations with money-changers, bankers, lawyers, architects, insurance agents, accountants, boards of trustees, dealers in secondhand automobiles and refrigerators, as well as in our relations with our coheirs, we are in the habit of suspecting fraud and of taking precautions.

Let us apply to our favorite newspaper the methods of verification which we are accustomed to apply to the reports of the persons mentioned above: no more will be needed to rid us of a large number of errors. When a businessman who wants my money waxes eloquent upon the stability and the strength of his business, promises that it will pay me considerable dividends under any and all circumstances, and denies that it has any weak points, I am not fool enough to put my trust in such an interested witness without being further informed. For complementary information I shall address myself to people who have no interest in his business and to people who are interested in rival businesses. In regard to each report, I shall ask myself if it is consistent, if it presents solid proofs, if it contains significant silences. After that, by comparing the documents, I shall arrive at a conclusion sufficiently founded to justify a resolute decision.

Why, then, are we more credulous when the question concerns the common welfare, when the honor, liberty, and lives of innumerable innocent persons are involved, than we are when what is involved is our personal affairs? In the course of conversation, someone called my attention to the case of a certain respectable and not uninfluential personage who believed in the authenticity of the Protocols of the Elders of Zion, and who did not fail to make use of them to further his propaganda. It was remarked that perhaps this man was acting in good faith: everyone knows that the Protocols are an obvious forgery, but the respectable personage had read in his favorite newspaper that they were authentic. He had not investigated further. In order to evaluate such a procedure, we have but to ask the following question: Had it been a document depriving him of a big estate, would he not have made certain of its authenticity more scrupulously?

The example of the Protocols reminds us that of all the ways of telling a lie, the most outspoken, the most brutal way is not always the least skillful. According to Hitler's celebrated saying, the ordinary man, who is accustomed to tell little lies, not big ones, suspects a lie when it is little but does not suspect it when it is enormous. To present a proposition whose falsity anyone can verify is a tactic which often succeeds. The reader tells himself that if the proposition were false it would be too easy to confound the proponents of it; he therefore concludes that it is true. Amongst the rules destined to protect our minds against falsehood, let us give first place to the following: Never admit that a proposition

is true simply because it would be easy to expose its erroneous-
ness if it were false.

After the frank falsehoods come the innumerable varieties
of masked falsehoods. It would be interesting to classify and
name the latter. Let us specify, as particularly important
and frequent, the variety characterized by an equivocal use
of words. Here, again, the success of the artifice is due to its
simplicity. To use a word in one of its meanings at the beginning of a train of reasoning, then to substitute another meaning of the same word, and to draw a conclusion which would
be true if the first meaning had been maintained, is an extremely flagrant sophism. The sophism is concealed by its
very flagrancy. People suppose that any self-respecting sophism will be subtle; they do not suspect a sophism in the
absence of all subtlety.

Finally, there is an artifice which, in a large number of
cases, permits one to obtain all the effects of a lie without
running any risk of being caught lying. It is the artifice of
partial truth, of truth selected, dosed. Here even the person
of good faith runs a great risk of being seduced by the practices of bad faith. He will not win his way clear unless his will
to honesty be exceptionally strong, vigilant, pure, and straight-
forward. If only because of lack of time and space, it is nearly
always impossible to say all that we know. Every story is an
abridgment. Every interpretative commentary implies a
choice amongst the innumerable causes and conditions of
the event to be interpreted. Furthermore, the publication of
certain truths under certain circumstances can be a vicious
thing. By publishing one truth we often run the risk of withdrawing attention from another truth. Now, to withdraw attention from a certain truth at the moment when justice
demands that that truth be present in every mind is an offense, sometimes an extremely grave offense, against justice
and against truth itself. Let us give a few examples.

At the time when the Armenians were being massacred by the Turks, it would have been criminal to call general attention to the wrongdoings of the Armenians, even those that were well established. Justice demanded that the world should talk about the wrongdoings of the Turks. At the time when religion was subjected to bloody persecution in Mexico, whoever emphasized what was wrong with Mexican clerics became an accomplice of Calles' murderous gang. At the time when only Great Britain's resistance could save the world from the most cruel of imperialisms, the propogandists who turned the attention of their readers to the faults of British imperialism were not motivated by a desire to do homage to truth—their purpose was to use certain truths as a screen to hide other truths. During the long agony of the Jews under the Nazi regime, anyone who drew attention to the faults of the Jews, even supposing that he limited himself to such faults as were proved, deserved to be regarded as an assassin of Jews, more cowardly and more odious than Hitler's specialized killers.

It must, then, be resolutely affirmed that it may be legitimate, that it may be indispensable, to keep silent in regard to certain truths, or at least to defer their publication until a later period. Is it possible to define a criterion which will permit one to distinguish between those truths which one shall leave unspoken and those which one shall not leave unspoken? ⌈The criteria currently in use are utilitarian—the choice between what is to be said and what is not to be said is determined by my interest, or the interest of the group with which I identify myself. ⌉But the authentic criterion is relative to that which outweighs all utility—the truth. In each of the examples cited above, it is truth itself which demands that certain truths be left unspoken, at least for a time. Published at the wrong season, they would constitute a screen against other, more pressing truths, and thereby would serve the cause of falsehood. Serve truth—by silence as well as by speech. This maxim does not lend itself to automatic application, like an algebraic formula. It is meaningless except to souls devoured by love of truth.

The Love of Truth Is Indivisible

The love of truth is the most natural thing in the world. Why, then, is it that, as a matter of fact, truth is so little loved? Let us not be satisfied with accusing the perversity of human nature. In the commerce of souls with truth, there are possibly certain systems of illusion, to expose which would suffice to deprive falsehood of some effective instruments.

To recall that there are divers kinds of truth, that the truth of a necessary proposition and that of a historical proposition, the truth of a theoretical proposition and that of a practical proposition, are different in nature, is but to repeat a commonplace. But in the order of moral and concrete psychology we have still much to learn concerning the consequences of this commonplace.

The diversity of truths conceals the unity of truth. Here is a psychological accident which occurs very frequently and is too little known. The natural tendency which carries our minds towards truth finds satisfaction in a certain realm of knowledge; satisfied, it stops there, and he who would give his life for a truth of a certain kind is found, in some other realm, to be indifferent to truth and falsehood. The absurdity of such a practice often remains concealed from the scrutiny of our consciences. For the absurdity to appear, the instinct for truth must show signs of being unappeased. Now it has found peace, it has illusorily satisfied its hunger, by acting in a limited field.

So it comes about that a positive scientist—a physicist, a chemist, a biologist—displays an admirable honesty in criticizing his own discoveries and theories, and a complete indifference in regard to the truths of metaphysics and religion. Nothing could be more edifying than his search for truth in the scientific field in which he is interested. If he suspects the presence of some factor which could make their meaning uncertain, he does not hesitate to regard experiments which have cost him years of work as null and void. His generalizations are exactly measured by the frequency of incontestably observed facts. He refuses himself the pleasure of indulging in brilliant but risky theories. He publishes little, because there are few results of which he is perfectly certain. Always ready to recognize his errors and the infinitesimal extent of his knowledge, he willingly bears the mockery of less scrupulous colleagues. What does he care for fame? His consciousness of scientific probity suffices him. That too happy consciousness allows him to pass a thoroughly agreeable life without concerning himself about truth and falsehood in fields removed from his specialty. Has God spoken? Does God exist? Our conscientious researcher turns away from such questions with a loftiness that expresses his sense of an incontestable right. Outside the field of his choice, truth has no further rights to the assent of his intellect. His intellect has all rights.

From the point of view defined by the object of his study, what is supremely important here is the monstrous but frequent association of a splendid intransigence in respect to religious, metaphysical, and moral truths, with a degrading indifference in respect to what we shall call historico-practical truth. (By this, I mean the entire aggregation of historical facts, whether recent or remote, which are of such a nature as to affect our attitudes as party men, our interests, our habitual tastes, and the esteem in which we hold the past. For example: Are the Protocols of the Elders of Zion authentic? Did Hitler save Germany and Austria from communism? Did the German air force bomb Guernica?) Here, as in the case of the scientist just described, the natural desire for truth is illusorily satisfied, then falls asleep, although truth demands that it remain awake. A sacrilegious paradox: [the desire for truth is illusorily satisfied with the most sublime of foods, and the mind refuses to perceive that the truth which has nourished it imposes upon it a sacred duty to seek truth in all things, without setting any limit to the rights of truth.]

finding truth in one thing shouldn't stop you from finding truth in everything.

Anyone who has understood in what a basic and absolute sense the possession of liberty is dependent upon submission to truth will recognize that the quality of a free man demands a love of truth which is not conditional and limited, but total and indivisible. In respect to things moral, social, and political, problems of truth can be reduced to the two systems which we have just mentioned: the system of religious, metaphysical, and moral truths, and the system of historico-practical truths. There must, then, in the daily life of a free man be moments wrested from business, from pleasures, from passions, from work, in which the mind withdraws into itself and strengthens its adherence to these two systems of truths. [The need to consecrate a certain time each day to meditation upon eternal truths is well known to all those who have had the benefit of an elevated moral discipline and of a spiritual education. But—especially if they have the dangerous responsibility of teaching others—let them not neglect to consecrate as well a time of generous attention to forming true judgments upon historical facts whose interpretation determines their attitudes in the development of temporal history] Love of truth remains authentic only so long as it remains undivided.

Freedom and Autonomy

However well we know that freedom is a divine name, we find it hard to prevent ourselves from treating it as a suspect person. Common experience, as well as history, has a great deal to say on the subject of its extravagances. In the eyes of a reasonable, thoughtful, prudent man any operation which promotes freedom is a risky one, and must be accompanied by guarantees against license, rebellion, and the misuse of freedom. These common-sense views are not false: they are unhappily incomplete. Unless we go beyond them in our dealings with freedom, we shall more than likely adopt an empirical and inconsistent course of conduct.

According to the felicitous terminology employed by Maritain in a well-known study,[2] mere free will, mere freedom of choice, has the character only of an initial freedom. It is freedom in its primitive, in its native state. Now, according to the law of progressiveness, which is the law of our whole nature, there is a great distance between the native state and the truly natural state, between the primitive condition in which a perfection exists only in a mixed and precarious form, and the terminal condition of a perfection that is stable and pure. Terminal freedom is not merely freedom of choice, but also freedom of autonomy. Here freedom of choice contains the possibility of making bad choices. Freedom of autonomy, in the measure in which it is actually realized, excludes that dreadful possibility. Freedom of autonomy is constituted by the presence of law within liberty. It is won by a process of interiorization of the law. At this point, in order to avoid misunderstanding, let us point out that the term *law*, here and in the following pages, refers either to

[2] *Freedom in the Modern World*, New York: Charles Scribner's Sons, 1936.

natural laws, which are not man-made, or to those man-made laws which are just. We take it for granted that an unjust law, having no connection with the principle of all law, is not a law at all. Let it not be objected that it is sometimes morally good, indeed obligatory, to obey an unjust law. When we feel obliged to obey an unjust law, it is generally because by disobeying it we should cause disorder and set an example which would be exploited against genuine laws by the spirit of disobedience; thus, we comply with a "law" which has no binding power in order not to disobey the obviously genuine and binding law that disobedience to laws should not be encouraged.

The wrong use of freedom occupies so large a place in our meditations that we have difficulty in preserving ourselves from the feeling that free will necessarily implies the possibility of doing wrong. Thus, a will whose adherence to the good should be infallible would have abdicated its freedom; and what, by an abuse of language, is called terminal freedom would be reduced to the necessity of willing the good— a privileged necessity, but in the long run one as foreign to freedom as, for example, the fidelity of vegetable life in following its cycles.

Such a concept contains a basic error fraught with consequences. Adherence to the good does not eliminate freedom of choice: within the limits of the good, numerous possibilities are still offered to our faculty of choosing. Far from eliminating freedom of choice, adherence to the good renders it perfect, *precisely as freedom of choice.* This is the point which it is important to understand. The object of the act of choosing is a means. Now, a bad means leads us away from our supreme end; in the final analysis, it is not a means because it does not lead to the end. There is only the appearance of a means and of an object of choice. To remove the possibility of a bad choice is simply to liberate free will from

a deceitful appearance and to restore to it its genuine object
—the veritable means, the means which leads to the end.
Terminal freedom includes a freedom of choice which has
attained to the purity of its idea.

An agent is said to be autonomous, in an absolute sense,
when it is identical with its law. This kind of autonomy belongs only to God. An agent is said to be autonomous, in a
relative but yet entirely proper sense, when its law, without
being identical to its being, dwells in it and governs it from
within, so that the spontaneous inclinations of the agent
coincide with the exigencies of the law. For creatures not
endowed with reasons, autonomy has the character of a
datum: it suffices that they are what they are for their tendencies to conform with their law. For reasonable creatures,
autonomy has the character of a vocation and a conquest. In
the native state, man's will is an indeterminate complex of
tendencies in which the order of nature will be established
only by the action of reason. So long as this imposition of
order remains unaccomplished, the law remains in some measure exterior to the will. The distance which separates it from
the will is manifested by conflicts and defeats. The faculty of
choosing is divided between the veritable means and the illusory means, which latter often carries off the victory. The
interiorization of the law is effected by an oscillating movement between two lines of progress, one of which consists in
an ever better understanding of what it is needful to know
in order to act rightly, the other in an ever-deepening, spontaneous, and voluntary adherence to the necessary ends of
our activity.

Thus, once the aspirations of free nature are precisely
understood, freedom ceases to present the appearance of a
fantastical and ambitious personage, always ready, if not duly
confined and repressed, to destroy order and arrest life; useful in critical periods, when there are obstacles to be over-

come, but little inclined to creative activity, and consequently not suitable for use in periods of construction or reconstruction. Freedom, correctly understood, is the most ordered thing in the world. It causes order to descend into the depths of the human will. This is the thing for which despotism will not forgive it. Collusions between despotism and anarchy, of which contemporary history furnishes so many examples, are a phenomenon easily comprehended. Despotism needs anarchy, in order that it may have a reason for existing: it cannot reign except over subjects refractory to autonomy, who call it to their aid, or at least tolerate it, because an external law is after all better than a total absence of law. The sure means of starving despotism out of existence is to realize, at all levels of personal and social life, the fusion of law and freedom—an operation which has nothing of the character of a compromise, since it brings both freedom and law to a state of perfection.

Slaves and Rebels

Like all beautiful and difficult things, the quest for autonomy is subject to perversions. The truly autonomous will is, properly speaking, no longer subjected to law, since law has become interior to it. To be freed from law: we have here an equivocal ideal. The road which leads to autonomy is long and laborious. How should we not be tempted to take a short cut? The practice of rebellion leads directly, without waiting and without effort, to a situation exactly opposite to the state of autonomy, yet productive of an intoxication in which the natural tendency of the free will towards autonomy finds an illusory satisfaction. Rebellion introduced into daily life is a covert attack against the way of life produced by freedom.

It would be useful to classify and characterize the different types of habitual rebels. At the foot of the ladder there are what the Marxists call the *Lumpenproletariat*, a miscellaneous collection of outcasts who, whether through misfortune or by their own fault, have not found a place in society and are in perpetual revolt against its institutions: vagabonds, thieves, beggars, the chronically jobless, prostitutes. Next come the individualistic petty bourgeois who are outraged by police regulations concerning the movement and parking of automobiles; suspicious farmers who hold that the value of their properties and the amount of their incomes are family secrets which no power on earth has the right to search out. Then come the feudatories of land, industry, and banking —adventurous, energetic, and proud, true descendants of the barons of old and, like the latter, strongly inclined to transform themselves into brigands by imperceptible transitions, irreconcilable enemies of social security, of minimum-wage laws, of all state supervision of business combines and the relations of capital and labor. Next come those intellectuals and artists whose passion to discover their ego and to express it has condemned them to a resentful solitude. Conceptual and esthetic refinement have deprived them of the moral comfort normally assured by participation in collective life and communication with universal nature; they are animated by an incessant desire for revenge upon the communities from which they have excluded themselves; manners and laws, laws of society and laws of nature, are equally odious to them. Finally, let us not fail to recognize the subtlest of all the varieties of rebels, those who hide their rebellion in the sublimity of an uncompromising ideal. We shall call them the perfectionists. They are usually disillusioned optimists. Weak souls inferior to their tasks, they understand confusedly that the little good which it is possible to realize in this world is bought at the price of incessant effort and at best exists only precariously. This effort they refuse to make, and they project their sublime ideal into the past, into a good old time whose virtues are univerifiable, into the conventional Middle Ages imagined at the dawn of the Romantic period by writers ill adapted to the modern world. They feel that they are invulnerable in their retrospective utopia; thence they direct their criticism against all the constructions of this present age, in which we are called upon to act with courage. They are to be ranked amongst the most dangerous of nihilists.

Let a catastrophe bring in the triumph of tyranny, and most of these rebels will willingly come to terms with it. Between the despot and the rebel there is a fundamental likeness which outweighs all their differences: both have a liking for the arbitrary. The great, the really significant dividing line does not exist between despot and rebel; it exists between those who love the arbitrary and those who hate it. The free man detests the arbitrary, in himself first of all, and then in others. Let us not lose sight of this order. We put ourselves on the wrong side of the dividing line—on the side of the despots, the rebels, and the slaves—each time that we reserve our indignation for arbitrary acts committed by others and neglect to observe the forces of arbitrariness which are perpetually welling up in ourselves.

Thus, an attitude of systematic ill will towards laws and regulations, a determination to regard all authority as a necessary evil which should be reduced to a minimum and to which, under any and all circumstances, one will refuse inner respect—these character traits of which individualistic peoples are so proud and which have often been cited as precious guarantees of freedom, appear to us to be nothing but obnoxious attitudes, well calculated to pave the way for despotism by making the practice of the arbitrary familiar to the minds of men. One truly detests arbitrariness only by loving and respecting just laws, regulations necessary for the com-

mon welfare, and legitimate authorities; by loving and respecting them to the point of giving any superior the benefit
of the doubt when we believe, without being certain, that he
is overstepping his true powers. When the abuse becomes
certain, when authority interferes in what does not concern
it, when an unjust law claims the prerogatives of a true law,
when men in power turn to their own profit the services
which are due only to the common welfare, the arbitrary
has no adversaries more inflexible than men whom inner
respect for authority has trained to fight against the arbitrary.

This should make it perfectly clear that the spirit of rebellion, which is at work under all circumstances and constantly
interferes with the operation of laws, has nothing in common with rightful resistance to tyranny.

The Community of the Free

It is trite to recall that every despotism owes its strength
to the disunion of its subjects. The spirit of rebellion maintains this disunion; each man practices rebellion in his own
way, according to principles which are his own. It is only
by accident, and in the most precarious fashion, that the
spirit of rebellion is accompanied by a community of principles and favors unity of action. The only precaution the
despot need take is to scatter his attacks. So long as the rebel
does not feel himself directly threatened, why should he take
the risks of resistance? And if the threat comes nearer, there
is every likelihood that he will be able to escape it by slipping
in amongst the beneficiaries of the situation.

Love of the laws, inner respect for authority and for those
who are invested with it, contribute most effectively towards
making the sense of the common welfare present in each
man's consciousness. The law is by its essence a rule relative
to the common welfare; authority, considered in its essential

function, is a specialized prudence in the pursuit of a welfare which is not individual, but common. The servile soul and the rebellious soul have no reason whatever for giving an inner assent to the laws and to authority; for them, it is enough to adopt, pragmatically, a course of conduct intended to avoid the principal disadvantages of disobedience. It is for the sake of the common welfare that the free man accords respect and love to laws and authorities. But, from that moment, he escapes from the solitude of the rebel. Inner, rational, virtuous submission proceeds from a principle which is the great factor of unity; this submission is the foundation of a community of free men.

The sense of the common welfare, cultivated into virtue by the inner practice of social discipline, does away with distances between the members of the community and makes it impossible for despotism to employ its favorite tactic, that of scattered attacks. If we have this sense of the common welfare, we understand that an arbitrary act directed against one of us is in reality directed against each of us and against our whole community. We shall not wait for the arbitrary to turn upon our own person, our private interests; as soon as it attacks the rights of one amongst us, it attacks that collective, unanimous, or communal life which is a thing within my soul and which is more precious to me than any private advantage. The supreme guarantee of liberty is the solidarity of free men in the common welfare.

It would be madness to believe that such a solidarity will be able to establish itself spontaneously in the hour of crisis. A solidarity improvised under the threat of a tyranny ready to devour everything will perhaps suffice to avoid utter disaster; it will accomplish even so much only at the cost of enormous losses. It is in the commerce of daily life that the solidarity of free men trains and strengthens itself to the point of discouraging any attempt at enslavement. Furthermore, the forces of despotism never relax, and the wrongs that they perpetrate in the silence of periods of apparent peace can equal, or exceed, the great destructions of periods of crisis. Let us look back for a moment at the days when in our old civilized societies there were neither concentration camps, nor racial laws, nor the one-party system, nor special courts, nor a Gestapo, nor total wars. According to the simplified picture the history books give us, these periods developed in a logical harmony, slightly troubled at times by sensational assassinations, minor wars, fires, epidemics, legal scandals, and revolts among the underfed. If one looks more closely, if one tries to understand the real condition of the great mutes of history, the working and the peasant classes, during these happy periods when nothing or almost nothing happened, one finds oneself confronted by an immensity of suffering, due in great part to acts of exploitation. There is not a day in the life of humanity on which there is not some occasion for the solidarity of free men to act against ever-recurring threats of abuse.

Here attention must be called to the privileged possibilities open to labor unions. In spite of numberless abuses, unionism remains the most fertile of the institutions designed to protect and to further freedom in our modern societies. It would be possible to cite many examples of perverse union action, oriented towards the satisfaction of group egoisms and the establishment of new oligarchies which are no strangers to the desire to exploit. Subject to corruption like all human institutions, the labor union has this privilege, that it cannot make the least concession to the spirit of exploitation without being false to its genetic idea and accepting all the disadvantages of a contradictory position. It is in its essence the instrument of a group of men who have renounced the easy advantages of servitude, the trickery of

egoism, and the disorders of rebellion, to link their fate
to that of their brothers in the disciplined pursuit of a freedom which is indissolubly the freedom of each and of all.
There is no room in a union—except by mistake—for a man
who sees no harm in his comrade's being ill paid if he himself gets a good wage; who does not take it to heart if his
comrade's contract is broken, because he believes that he
himself will always be able to "fix things" so that he can
hold his job; who redoubles his flattery of his employers
when he knows that arbitrariness is on the increase. There
is no room in a union for an individualist determined to
follow his own judgment under all circumstances. Émile
Durkheim, who despite his system was in certain senses a
profound moralist, used to say in his jargon that contemporary societies had the misfortune to be *anomous.* An
anomous society provides excellent material for a despotism,
which undertakes to give it a dose of order by means of
police, spies, and terrorism. It is nowise surprising that despotism has a particular aversion for labor unions and similar
organizations; for it is precisely there that the centers of
growth of an autonomous society are to be found.

The history of the working-class movement offers the spectacle of a conflict of tendencies well calculated to instruct us
in the directions which should be taken by an institution
desirous of accomplishing autonomy rather than of dissipat-
ing its strength in enterprises of rebellion. According to a
certain concept of unionism, a labor union is simply an association of employees united in defense of their interests. Its
function is to restore equality in transactions relating to wages
and hours of work, to health conditions in factories, to transportation facilities, and so forth. The opposing concept is far
more ambitious. It includes a definite ethics of the laboring
life, it includes a systematic view of the historic mission of

the working-class movement as a factor in general changes in modern societies, it includes an ambition to abolish the solitude of the proletarian and to supplant the demoralizing dispersion of the individualistic epoch by new forms of community life in which the worker would find at once a sense of security and a sense of devotion. This ambition gives birth to a number of enterprises which have only a distant connection, or no connection at all, with problems of wages and working conditions—mutual-assistance societies, consumers' cooperatives, institutes for popular education, factory committees, autonomous workshops, and so forth.

Let us now picture to ourselves the psychological situation which the former concept is likely to create amongst unionists. Specialized in the task of making demands, constantly irritated in accomplishing their task by the resistance of employers' organizations, having hardly any opportunity to acquire an experience of the realities of the creative order, finding almost no encouragement save in successes forcibly wrested from those in authority, these unionists will be strongly tempted to become "perpetual rebels."

The ambitious concept of union action tends to create an entirely different psychology. The unionist is no longer a man whose specialty is making demands. The fight to obtain demands is only a part of his activity, the experience of class conflicts is only a part of his social experience. Cooperatives, institutes for popular education, antonomous workshops, are not things which can be founded and operated by merely curbing powers of oppression, to overcome obstacles, or to master wills which seek to restrain. The foundation and above all the operation of such organizations demand personal and social discipline, the spirit of sacrifice, authority and obedience, a clear-sighted experience of economic and social realities, patience, and fidelity—all of which are attitudes conducive to shunning the arbitrary and the utopian, and to raising within the will a structure of habitual submission to the laws of nature and of society.

These reflections upon the union movement are intended to illustrate the general laws of the quest for autonomy as it should be pursued in the humble and fruitful tasks of daily life. Let us attempt to restate these laws in a few clear formulas.

1. The quest for autonomy must above all eschew any form of individualism. Autonomy is nothing but the climax of a process of interiorizing the law. The law is a rule of action whose object is the common welfare. Any will to emancipation which is foreign to the sense of the common welfare is directed towards anomy rather than towards autonomy.

2. It follows that it is not in solitude but in the community that the quest for autonomy should be pursued. My law will not become interiorized in me unless our law becomes interiorized in us. To want my autonomy without wanting that of my companions and that of our community is nonsense.

3. The winning of autonomy implies a resistance to all forms of despotism. It implies also, and most of all, the creation of an order interior to the things set in order, after the fashion in which natural laws are interior to things of nature, and the virtues to the virtuous will. The important thing is to unite in living institutions forces of resistance and creative energies.

4. Group egoism is not less destructive than individual egoism. In insisting upon the community character of the quest for autonomy, we must keep in mind not only the necessarily limited group which exists in our own vicinity —my family, my club, my union, my country—but also the whole hierarchy of larger and larger communities, whose boundaries coincide with those of all humanity. It is only upon the condition of submitting oneself to an absolute uni-

versalism and of accepting all the subordinations required by the universal order, that the quest for autonomy avoids degenerating into rebellion.

Many confusions will be cleared up, many psychological difficulties will cease to appear insoluble, when the men who represent the cause of freedom cease to express themselves with systematic suspicion in respect to authority. [Reduced to its essence, authority, as we have already said, is only the prudence of society on its road towards the common welfare.] It is neither a necessary evil nor a lesser good. It is a thing good purely and simply—as wisdom, reason, and order are good. It is the basic principle of the right direction and distribution of activities in the life of the community. Its connection with the common welfare is so evident that it is impossible to treat it with suspicion without jeapardizing the sense of community and entering upon the road of individualistic revolt. It is a matter of pure accident—however frequently the accident may occur—that authority develops into arbitrariness. On the contrary, a fixed attitude of opposition to authority is, essentially and not accidentally, the work of an arbitrary will. We have recognized in the arbitrary the supreme enemy of freedom.

A Universalist Ethics

In our times, the winning of freedom has the character of a renaissance, of a reconstruction, of a renewal. The first thing to be done is to reverse the historical movement which has led so many peoples into slavery. Despite the military defeats and the losses of prestige suffered by the Nazis and their allies, this movement is still in progress in large portions of our societies.

Every reconstructive effort should draw inspiration from

the lessons of the decadence. The experience of enslavement has taught us that the servile soul is the soul which has lost its self-respect. If we understand how such a disaster is brought about, we shall in all likelihood understand under what conditions we shall succeed in recovering the souls of free men.

We have had the privilege of being born into societies in which the influence, whether direct or indirect, of true religion informs every man of the strictly infinite and eternal value of every reasonable being. Common immorality often produces a state of degradation which is fatal to our sense of our own dignity. But it would be an extremely naïve error to believe that only common immorality can produce a loss of self-respect. Let us look within ourselves, let us look around us: many people whose behavior is said to be irreproachable—chaste, temperate, frugal people—have souls which are nonetheless the souls of slaves. How does one lose one's self-respect whilst remaining a decently behaved person? Here is a problem which certainly is worth the trouble of elucidating.

By reason of the unity of essence which confers on all men an equal fundamental dignity, the sense of human dignity is indivisibly concerned with all men; it suffers a serious and decisive wrong every time it accommodates itself to an exception. However, there is an order of proximity and remoteness in our relations with our kind; the Christian expression, *neighbor*, reminds us, even as we apply it to men the most distant, that we owe a predilection to those who are nearest to us. It is normal and right that I should feel more keenly an outrage upon my brother than an outrage upon a person less closely allied to me, although they are both my neighbors. An imperceptible deviation suffices to sink the extreme periphery of the human universe into nothingness. If it is true that I owe more consideration to my neighbors than to those

who live far from me, it is easy to imagine that, beyond a
certain radius, I owe mankind no consideration whatsoever.
If it is true that I must take more and more interest in men
as they are nearer and nearer to me, have I not the right to
conclude that at a very great distance from the center of my
interest men are no longer interesting at all? Little by little
the circle grows smaller. At each turning of lived history,
new fractions of humanity are ejected beyond the frontiers
of my moral sense. I have no notion that I am in danger of
being swallowed up in turn in the growing multitude of those
men to whom I refuse my respect. By the most fatal of illusions, I feel myself more and more filled with respect for
myself. In reality, by refusing my respect to men who do not
touch me sufficiently, I have left alive in myself, in regard to
myself, only feelings of egoism.

It is by restoring an integrally universalist ethics that we
shall reverse the movement which has reduced so many souls
to slavery. Let there be no misunderstanding: there is an apparent universalism which combines a burning interest in
men who live at great distances from ourselves with a comfortable indifference in respect to those who are nearest to us.
There is not much that we can do for the former; consequently, to be on fire with love for them presents no difficulties. We can do a great deal for the latter, but at the price
of costly sacrifices. True universalism accomplishes, within
order, a fusion of the love of the nearest and the love of the
farthest. We love our children better after having learned to
love them in the persons of Chinese, Polish, Jewish, Russian,
and German children. I desire justice for my brothers more
energetically after having learned to desire it for an innocent
man sentenced to prison on the other side of the world. I
have more respect for my dignity as a man after having
learned to respect man in the person of a criminal subjected
to punishments not provided for by the law.

To reduce our moral universe by refusing to interest ourselves in those who live far away from us is to free ourselves from a great weight of cares and anxieties; to reserve our love and our indignation for the faraway human being whom we cannot possibly help is to simplify our task to a remarkable extent. An integral and properly ordered universalism has its unpleasant side: it excludes any simplifications, it multiplies our cares, and kills our desire to enjoy life. The burden that it lays upon us is heavier than ever in this century when speedy communications and the wide diffusion of news expose us to the sufferings of all mankind. The old Christian idea of a human republic under the rule of God, *Res publica sub Deo,* forces itself upon our minds with a cogency but recently unsuspected. A free man's conscience is as wide as the world.

2

Liberty and Authority

DURING THE FIRST YEARS of the post-World War I period and under the cover of a reaction of "sane thinking" against the errors of liberalism, the idea of liberty itself was derided.* A good deal of social success was assured to those who expressed their contumely in some particularly crude and grossly ironical way. The style of the new fashion was given by the widely cheered statement of Mussolini, boasting of the readiness of Fascism "to trample upon the more or less decomposed body of the Goddess of Liberty."

This is the way that history proceeds to the liquidation of great errors. As the masses were becoming disgusted with the deceptions of liberalism, educated people, to whom was entrusted the custody of invaluable truths accidentally linked to pernicious errors, let the things go—nay, added to the im-

* This chapter originally appeared in the *Proceedings of the American Catholic Philosophical Association*, vol. 16 (1940), pp. 86–114.

patience of the masses the wickedness of their ideological fanaticism. A divine name was crushed together with the rotten corpse of an ambiguous goddess. Among the "intellectuals" who danced an infernal dance around the spot, there were some people accustomed to pay lip service, and possibly more, to St. Thomas.

The Meaning of Liberty

Yet, all the teaching of St. Thomas shows that liberty is an absolute perfection, *perfectio simpliciter simplex,* which can be attributed to God in a formal sense. Recall the highly intelligible distinction made by metaphysicians between the perfections of being whose concept necessarily implies some imperfection (*perfectiones mixtae,* mixed perfections) and those perfections whose concept does not imply any imperfection.[1] The world of our experience, empirically considered, does not show anything but imperfect realizations of the perfections of being. Just as our biological life, which involves all the imperfections bound up with materiality, so our intellect is an essentially imperfect thing, a power doomed to acquire painstakingly and step by step limited cognitions whose possession always remains precarious. The difference will not become manifest unless the analogical insight of metaphysics is substituted for the short-sightedness of the empirical consideration. From a metaphysical point of view, things of the observable world have in themselves, at the core of their imperfect entity, perfections that can be abstracted from any imperfect realization without their essential constitution being impaired in any way. An idea like that of

[1] On the theory of the absolute perfections of being, see Garrigou-Lagrange, *God, His Existence and His Nature, First Part;* M. T.-L. Penido, *Le Rôle de l'analogie en théologie dogmatique* (Paris, 1931), Ch. 1; J. Le Rohellec, *Problemes philosophiques* (Paris, 1933), I, Ch. 4.

biological life is not capable of such a treatment; forcibly abstracted from the imperfections that it connotes, it disappears altogether. If I consider, on the contrary, such a thing as the intellect of man, I recognize in it the transcendent essence of the intellect, which essence, far from being necessarily bound up with the limitations of its human realization, aspires to a condition where it could get rid of them and assert itself completely. I understand that the intellect is infinitely more truly an intellect without the limitations imposed on it by material existence, or, more generally, created existence. In the same way, the truth that human knowledge is capable of is partial and precarious, the justice that the human heart is capable of is a poor justice, ceaselessly jeopardized by opposite forces. But I understand that truth and justice are infinitely more identical with themselves, realize more genuinely and more formally their idea, in an infinite existence. The intellect, truth, justice, are absolute perfections of being and divine names.

When the ethical point of view replaces the metaphysical one, some absolute perfections present in man give rise to a conflict and to a most difficult problem. On the one hand, inasmuch as they are absolute perfections and divine names, nothing is more desirable than to have them increase and flourish to the utmost capacities of human nature. On the other hand, since their realization in man is bound up with many imperfections and risks, there may be a chance that, by cherishing them and fostering them without discrimination, we might have the imperfections involved outpace their development and overwhelm them, the final result being sheer destruction. Take, for example, the virtue of mercy: it is the most lovable of the divine names; but human mercy is psychologically connected with temperamental and emotional dispositions which may very well mislead and corrupt our will for mercy. An indiscriminate exaltation of mercy turns almost fatally to a predominance of an ambiguous sentimentality at the expense of justice and fortitude, finally at the expense of mercy itself. The example of mercy is more striking since mercy is a virtue, an indefectible principle of right action, *of which nobody can make wrong use.* [The problem appears much more difficult when the absolute perfection is of such a nature that its human realization can be used for evil. Such is the case with science or art. Such is the case, above all, with liberty.]

In order to approach a solution, the first thing to do is to disentangle ideally the divine perfection from the dubious drives with which it is associated in the concreteness of our empirical existence. The idea that liberty results from a lack of determination, that it results from the sheer absence of a positive determination, that it is, in short, less than a univocal determination, is frequent among scientists and philosophers. I can think of a physicist who wrote that an example of free action could be found in the sudden and entirely indeliberate occurrence of a word to the mind of one concentrating upon a task which has nothing to do with the occurring word. This is what sound philosophy considers as a typical example of a chance event, understanding thereby an event that has no proper cause, no essential determination and that merely results from the meeting of an ununified plurality of causal lines. The fact that any deliberation is excluded from the example mentioned suggests that to confuse liberty with a lack of determination is to misunderstand radically and paradoxically its nature. [That liberty takes place in deliberate actions rather than in indeliberate happenings is an unquestionable datum of spontaneous consciousness.]

The same identification of liberty with a lack of determination is found in a number of literary works where happy life is conceived as a continual refusal to make decisive choices, an endless succession of experiments in which the person never engages himself fully, so as to preserve and ceaselessly increase the treasury of his possibilities. [Refusing to be determinately anything, trying everything without letting ourselves be steadily determined in any way, we should achieve an ability to become everything, and this ability which has the taste of the infinite, is understood to be the supreme liberty. It is easy to recognize in that description what philosophers technically call the potential indifference of the will, the passive indifference of the will, an indifference which is a state of non-achievement, a state of potency, *indifferentia potentialitatis*; an indifference which results from an ontological poverty: anything is good to one who has nothing.] Far from being identical with liberty, this indifference is an obstacle that liberty has to overcome in order to assert itself. The psychological name of passive indifference is *irresolution.*

Turning again to the data of spontaneous consciousness, it is entirely plain that freedom is most inescapably experienced when we feel that we are dominating over or mastering a situation. The Bergsonian conception of freedom, in spite of the effort made by its author to have it solely based on an experience of consciousness, is at variance with some unquestionable data of consciousness. If the Bergsonian view were true, I should enjoy the most striking experience of my liberty when my action proceeds from the whole of my psychical organism.[2] As a matter of fact, my best

[2] H. Bergson, *Time and Free Will,* translated by F. L. Pogson (London: Allen, [1910]), p. 165: "Therefore, it is only an inaccurate psychology, misled by language, which will show the soul determined by sympathy, aversion, or hate as though by so many forces pressing upon it. These feelings, provided that they go deep enough, each make up the whole soul, since the whole content of the soul is reflected in each of them. To say that the soul is determined under the influence of any one of these feelings is thus to

awareness of my freedom does not take place when the whole of my tendencies bear me smoothly in a certain direction. The realization of our liberty forces itself most conspicuously upon our consciousness when our psychical organism is divided by a conflict of tendencies. Imagine, for instance, a man who, after many years devoted to laziness, easy life and sensuous pleasures, has recently undergone a moral conversion. A conflict arises between his newly acquired moral convictions and his wrong habits which are still far from being uprooted. Let us suppose that the virtuous will overcomes passionate drives and imposes on them the rule of morality. At the very moment when this triumph occurs, he feels and realizes his freedom more decidedly than at any other time. Yet, such a free decision is not the expression of the whole person: passional drives, deeply rooted habits, are indeed voluminous parts of the personal organism. *Freedom means mastery rather than totality.*

This way we are led to understand that the identification of freedom with a lack of determination was due to the similarity in name of two notions which are sharply opposed to one another, although they are connected by the tie of a thin analogy. There is an indifference which results from a lack of determination, from an ontological poverty, from a state of potency, an indifference of potentiality. A subject which lacks determination, which is unachieved and thereby *open to* several possibilities is indifferent to the special nature of each of them. On the other hand, there is an indifference which is based upon the achievement of a being, the fullness of its determination, an indifference to

recognize that it is self-determined." P. 172: "In short, we are free when our acts spring from our whole personality, when they express it, when they have indefinable resemblance to it which one sometimes finds between the artist and his work. It is no use asserting that we are then yielding to the all-powerful influence of our character. Our character is still ourselves."

several possibilities which results from the higher actuality of a cause, its plenitude, its superabundance.[3] Active indif-

[3] On the twofold indifference of the will, see St. Thomas, *Contra Gentes*, 1, 82. In this article St. Thomas discusses the following objection against the thesis that God does not will necessarily things distinct from Himself: every power which is *ad utrumlibet* is in some way in potency, "nam *ad utrumlibet* species est possibilis contingentis"; but the divine will, since it is identical with the divine substance, cannot admit of any potency.—The answer is based on an explanation of the twofold meaning of the expression *ad utrumlibet*. "Ad utrumlibet enim esse alicui virtuti potest convenire dupliciter: Uno modo, ex parte sui; alio modo, ex parte ejus ad quod dicitur.— Ex parte quidem sui, quando nondum consecuta est suam perfectionem, per quam ad unum determinetur; unde hoc in imperfectionem virtutis redundat, et ostenditur esse potentialitas in ipsa, sicut patet in intellectu dubitantis, qui nondum assecutus est principia ex quibus ad alterum determinetur.—Ex parte autem ejus ad quod dicitur, invenitur aliqua virtus ad utrumlibet esse, quando perfecta operatio virtutis a neutro dependet, sed tamen utrumque esse potest; sicut aliquis, qui diversis instrumentis uti potest aliqualiter ad idem opus perficiendum. Hoc autem ad imperfectionem virtutis non pertinet, sed magis ad ejus eminentiam, in quantum utrumlibet oppositorum excedit, et ob hoc determinatur ad neutrum, sed ad utrumlibet se habet." See also *Sum. Theol.* 1a, q. 19, a. 4, ad 5. The most complete exposition of the question is found in John of St. Thomas *Cursus Philosophicus, Phil. Nat.*, IV, 12, 2 (Marietti ed., 3, p. 387 b, 12). "Indifferentia enim est duplex, alia passiva sive potentialitatis, alia activa sive potestatis. *Prima* est imperfecta et non conducit ad agendum, sed magis obest. Quanto enim aliquid magis est potentiale ad plura et indeterminatum, magis elongatur ab agendo et indiget determinari et actuari, ut de facto operatur. Quare ista indifferentia potentialitatis non est de ratione liberi, sed si invenitur in agente libero, est imperfectionis, quia non est sufficienter in actu, et ita quanto magis tollitur et removetur ista potentialitas, tanto magis perficitur libertas, quia reducitur ad actum.—At vero *potentia activa* seu potestatis adhuc est duplex: Quaedam est indifferentia solum *per modum universalitatis in agendo*, quatenus aliqua causa est aequivoca, et non solum unum effectum agere potest, sed etiam plures et diversae speciei. Et hoc etiam potest inveniri in causis necessariis; nam etiam sol plura potest agere, et sensus et intellectus plures actus elicere. Alia est *indifferentia dominativa* seu arbitrativa, quae ita habet eminentiam ad agenda plura, quod non potest obligari et coarctari ad agendum, sed potest agere vel non agere. Et hanc indifferentiam dicimus con-

ference does not always mean liberty: cognitive powers are actively indifferent inasmuch as they are capable of eliciting a multiplicity of acts virtually infinite in quality, however they are necessitated. Liberty represents an excellent degree of active indifference, an active indifference that goes so far as to imply not only the sheer capacity of eliciting actions qualitatively diverse, but also a domination over the attractive aspect of any possible action. Liberty is a dominating indifference most essentially constituted by the power of acting or refraining from acting, all things being the same.

As soon as this capital distinction between the two indifferences is understood, it immediately appears nonsensical to assume that the element of contingency, indetermination

---

sistere in hoc, quod non solum habeat potestatem super actum seu effectum, ad quem movet, sed etiam super judicium, a quo movetur, ita quod in manu sua habeat discernere et judicare et avertere illud judicium, a quo movetur, quod quia non habet brutum, cujus appetitus non potest avertere judicium semel positum, ideo caret libertate." *Cursus Theologicus*, 1–11, VI, Disp. 3, 28 (Vives ed., vol. 5, p. 373). "Est enim duplex indifferentia in nobis, altera dominii et universalitatis potentiae, quatenus voluntas est potens super plures actus, et super cessationem ab eis, et sic habet indifferentiam, seu universalitatem ad illos, et sic opponitur coarctationi, et coactioni ad unum ex parte potestatis operandi; et haec indifferentia si tollitur, perit libertas. Alia est indifferentia suspensionis, quasi indeterminatio, aut perplexitas, et haec se habet per modum potentialitatis, et imperfectionis, quando scilicet aliquis non afficitur magis ad unam partem quam ad aliam, vel si afficitur, parum curat, vel etiam hic et nunc individualiter non se determinat, sed in potentia se habet ad operandum: et haec indifferentia potentialis est imperfecta, et impedit operari, quia quamdiu aliquis est in hoc statu, non se resolvit, et sic non operatur. Determinatio ergo, seu resolutio hujus indifferentiae non tollit libertatem, sed juvat, et reducit in actum, et ad hoc ponitur praedeterminatio physica, quae non est aliud, quam resolutio indifferentiae suspensivae, et perplexitatis, quatenus haec resolutio non fit solum ab objecto alliciente, et judicio proponente, quae est moralis motio, sed etiam ex parte Dei intus operantis, et inspirantis voluntatem, quae est physica operatio."

and chance—which is, in fact, inherent in human conduct —is of the essence of liberty. The only contingency that liberty metaphysically involves lies on the side of the effect, that may or may not be brought about. On the side of the agent liberty is compatible with the utmost necessity— better: liberty is not absolute unless the existence of the agent is absolutely necessary. The free acts of God are identical with the divine existence, whose necessity is absolute. The freedom of God is infinite precisely because, the being of God necessarily possessing its ultimate perfection, the divine will cannot feel any need, and enjoys an absolute indifference in regard to anything really distinct from the being of God. The most radical contingency on the side of things creatable corresponds to, and results from, the eternally necessary satisfaction of the divine desire.[4]

We now understand that even in the poorest of its forms, the form it has in man in his present life, the freedom of the will must be characterized as the outcome of an excess of ontological determination. The absolute freedom of God proceeds from the absolute necessity of the divine perfection, from the absolutely necessary achievement of the divine being. A free cause is a superdetermined cause.[5]

[4] "[St. Thomas] docet habitudinem ad volita creata non esse necessariam in Deo, et quod determinatur a se non aliunde, nec quasi in potentia existens ad aliquid, sed ex eo quod habet ex se necessitatem. Mirum dictum! Quod idem immutabile et necessarium in se existens fundet habitudinem contingentem ad aliud, quia ex se necessitatem habet." John of St. Thomas, *Cursus Theologicus*, 1, 19, Disp. 4, 48 (Vives ed., vol. 3, p. 251).

[5] "A cette potentialité dans toutes les choses créées et par conséquent dans tous les biens créées répondra l'indifférence dominatrice de la volonté, qui étant spécifiée par le bien comme tel (et ne pouvant donc dès qu'elle s'exerce, rien vouloir sans tendre d'abord à un bien choisi comme absolu), donne elle-même efficacité au bien particulier que l'intelligence lui présente et qui la détermine, parce qu'elle fait surabonder sur ce bien particulier, par lui-même absolument incapable de déterminer, le trop-plein de détermination qu'elle tient de

So far as ethics is concerned, the great trouble is that both kinds of indifference really exist in the structure of the will. Inasmuch as the will necessarily adheres to the absolute of the good presented by reason, the will is actively and dominatingly indifferent, it is free. On the other hand, there is in the human will an element of uncertainty, indecision, irresolution, potentiality, that St. Thomas compares with doubt in the intellect. Let it be understood that the development in man of the divine perfection constituted by freedom means, in the first place, that the mastery of the will, its strength, its resolution, its superdetermination, prevails over its being passively open to a number of possibilities.

On the ground of those considerations, we should assert that any form of social life which increases the lonesomeness of the individual, puts him in a state of doubt, makes it more difficult for him to come to decisions, is highly suspect of materializing an illusory conception of liberty. Conversely, liberty is promoted by any social background and environment that gives the individual more firmness, more cool-headedness, more self-control, more clear-sightedness, a more lucid insight into his own aspirations and the end he has to pursue.

The most serious imperfection of human freedom, of course, lies in its ability to choose evil. As a matter of fact, many people fail to realize that the freedom of choosing

---

son objet nécessaire, du bien comme tel; elle le fait gratuitement être bon purement et simplement pour le sujet, à cause, si l'on peut dire, de la plénitude de détermination intelligible dont elle regorge. Ainsi le principe de raison ne joue nulle part plus magnifiquement que dans le cas du libre-arbitre." J. Maritain, *Sept leçons sur l'être* (Paris: Téqui, 1934), p. 114.

It can be surmised that many difficulties concerning the use of the notion of causality in moral sciences would vanish if this expression "superdetermined causality" might become current and remove the fantastic idea of a liberty identified with a center of contingency and chance.

is not taken away, nay, is exalted when there is no longer any freedom of making a wrong choice. In order to remove the idea that the capacity of making wrong choices is essential to freedom,[6] we have to concentrate our attention

---

[6] St. Thomas, *De Veritate*, q. 24, a. 1 ad 16. "Si tamen aliqua creatura immobiliter adhaeret Deo, non propter hoc privatur libero arbitrio: quia potest adhaerendo multa facere vel non facere." *Ibid.* a. 3, ad 2. "Posse eligere malum, non est de ratione liberi arbitrii; sed consequitur liberum arbitrium secundum quod est in natura creata possibili ad defectum." *Sum. Theol.* 1a, q. 19, a. 10, ad 2. "Impossibile est eum [God] malum culpae velle. Et tamen ad opposita se habet, inquantum velle potest hoc esse, et non esse. Sicut et nos non peccando, possumus velle sedere et non velle sedere." *Ibid.* 1a, q. 62, a. 8, ad 2 (about freedom in blessed angels). "Virtutes rationales se habent ad opposita in illis ad quae non moventur naturaliter; sed quantum ad illa ad quae naturaliter ordinantur, non se habent ad opposita. Intellectus enim non potest non assentire principiis naturaliter notis; et similiter voluntas non potest non assentire bono inquantum est bonum, quia in bonum naturaliter ordinatur sicut in suum objectum. Voluntas enim angeli se habet ad opposita, quantum ad multa facienda vel non facienda; sed quantum ad ipsum Deum, quem vident esse ipsam essentiam bonitatis, non se habent ad opposita; sed secundum ipsum ad omnia diriguntur, quodcumque oppositorum eligant, quod sine peccato est." *Ibid.*, ad 3. "Liberum arbitrium sic se habet ad eligendum ea quae sunt ad finem, sicut se habet intellectus ad conclusiones. Manifestum est autem quod ad virtutem intellectus pertinet, ut ad diversas conclusiones procedere possit, secundum principia data. Sed quod in aliquam conclusiones procedat praetermittendo ordinem principiorum, hoc est ex defectu ipsius. Unde quod liberum arbitrium diversa eligere possit, servato ordine finis, hoc pertinent ad perfectionem ejus. Sed quod eligat aliquid, divertendo ab ordine finis, quod est peccare, hoc pertinet ad defectum libertatis. Unde major libertas arbitrii est in angelis qui peccare non possunt, quam in nobis qui peccare possumus." *Ibid.* 11a 11ae, q. 88, a. 4, ad 1 (answering the objection that the vow removes freedom, a gift of God). "Sicut non posse peccare non diminuit libertatem, ita etiam necessitas firmatae voluntatis in bonum non diminuit libertatem, ut patet in Deo et in beatis et talis est necessitas voti, similitudinem quamdam habens cum confirmatione beatorum." *Ibid.* 111a, q. 18, a. 4, ad 3. "Voluntas Christi, licet sit determinata ad bonum, non tamen est determinata ad hoc vel ad illud bonum. Et ideo pertinet ad Christum eligere per liberum arbitrium confirmatum in bono, sicut ad beatos."

again upon freedom as a power so determined, so actual, so eminent, that it dominates over a plurality of possibilities in the pursuit of its end. It must be kept in mind that the end as such is not the object of any choice. Choice, *electio,* is concerned with means; if it occurs that things which are really more than mere means fall under our choice, it is because those things although enjoying in some respect the value of ends, have something of the nature of the means (intermediary ends) and are taken by us as means inasmuch as they lead to some ulterior term. The only end which is unmistakably given by nature is the ultimate end abstractly considered in its form, *bonum in communi,* the good as such. So long as we have no concrete intuition of the reality in which the ultimate end of man consists, everything appears to us as means to the achievement of the only end that we unmistakably know by nature. Thus the range of our choice extends even to the concrete ultimate end and here lies the supreme infirmity of our freedom. Since freedom is a power of choosing the means within the limits defined by the end, any condition that puts at stake the end itself is profoundly in conflict with the very essence of freedom. The better the *ordo finis* is *servatus,* the better liberty is achieved. To take a homely example: the end being to reach the other shore of the ocean, I can choose between several transportation lines. The range of my freedom is limited by the attainment of this end, reaching the other shore of the ocean. Now, let us imagine that one of the lines is so unsafe that if I take it, I shall reach the bottom of the ocean rather than the other shore. *Is it not entirely plain that the removal of such a possibility, far from impairing my freedom, delivers it from its heaviest burden?*

The absolute character of the divine freedom proceeds from the perfect way in which the *ordo finis* is assured in

God. In the blessed soul the similarity to God reaches its highest degree; here also the *ordo finis* is perfectly assured by the vision of God which entirely eradicates any possibility of deviation from the end. There is no formal freedom in the act of beatific love by which the blessed soul indefectibly adheres to the supreme good. Yet it is significant, that John of St. Thomas ascribes to the beatific love what he calls an *eminent* freedom.[7] The blessed soul is not free to repress its love for the supreme good clearly seen. Nevertheless it would not be fitting to say that it *lacks* freedom in this indefectible adherence to the supreme end. The act of beatific love is not below the level of freedom, but above it. It is a perfect realization of that which constitutes the very source of the freedom of the will. Similarly, the perception of the self-evident principles is not formally scientific, since science deals with demonstrated conclusions; but it would not occur to anybody to say that the Understanding of Principles is unscientific or *lacks* the scientific character. The Understanding of Principles is not below but above the level of scientific knowledge. It is the

[7] John of St. Thomas, *Cursus Theologicus*, I-II, VI, Disp. 3, 28 (Vives ed., vol. 5, p. 370). "Quando autem dicimus dari liberum formaliter, et liberum eminenter, quod tamen in re necessarium est, intelligimus quod liberum formaliter est illud, quod procedit cum formali indifferentia, et contingentia, et sine ulla necessitate, ita quod possit non procedere, sicut communiter operamur libere. Liberum autem eminenter est illud, quod sine tali indifferentia formali, sed cum necessitate, non tamen orta ex coactione, vel coarctatione potentiae, sed ex adequatione totius universalitatis potentiae in agendo procedit. Quia enim radix libertatis in nobis oritur ex universalitate ipsius potentiae ad omne ens, seu ad omne bonum, inde est, quod quamdiu stat voluntatem operari ex ista universalitate stat operari libertate, quia universalitas illa indifferentiam importat, seu radicem indifferentiae; sed tamen ista indifferentia, et universalitas ita se habent, quod respectu boni limitati, et non adaequantis totam potentiae universalitatem operatur cum indifferentia, et libertate formali; respectu autem boni universalissimi, et summi, sicut est Deus clare visus, adaequatur tota universalitas, et indifferentia voluntatis."

source from which the scientific demonstration flows: it is eminently scientific. The more unshakable the understanding is, the better are the chances of achieving a satisfactory demonstration. Any failure to perceive the principles stultifies the demonstrative endeavor. A firmer adherence to the principles increases in every respect and does not diminish in any way the strength of the mind in its search for a conclusion. [In the same manner a firmer adherence to the end represents an unqualified improvement of the freedom of the will.] Although a state of indefectibility can not be achieved here below, it is possible for man to have his adherence to the ends of human life confirmed, under God, by grace and by infused and acquired virtues. At the ideal term of the moral and spiritual progress the freedom of man reaches a state of *sanctity*, that is, a state of purity and firmness. The freedom of making wrong choices is, as far as possible, removed, the freedom of choosing is unimpaired. The predominant inclinations of the will no longer conflict, but spontaneously agree with the precepts of the law; the law has become interior to the will. Terminal freedom is both freedom of choice and autonomy.[8] In such a condition of sanctity this divine name, freedom, becomes as resplendent as it can be in any creature within the limits of this perishable world.

Mutatis mutandis, what holds for the freedom of the individual holds also for the freedom of the group. There is such a thing as a dominating indifference in the mastery that a free society exercises over its own course of action. Just as there is in the individual will a burden of potentiality that the superdeterminated power of free choice must remove, so there are in the life of the group a number of factors which puzzle and weaken the common will, and

[8] See J. Maritain, *Freedom in the Modern World* (London: Sheed and Ward, 1935), Ch. 1.

those factors have to be overcome if the common will is to assert its mastery. Just as the personal freedom of choice is exalted by the removal of the *indifference of potentiality*, so the freedom of the group is exalted by the suppression of the disorderly forces that tend to make impossible a resolute course in common action. Finally, it is perfectly evident that the freedom of the group is not any more bound up with the possibility of making wrong choices than the freedom of the individual. There is such a thing as an interiorization of the law by the social body. Just as an individual person, through virtue, protects himself against the risk of making wrong choices, so a group, a society, a political body, may effectively strengthen its loyalty to the common good by the incorporation into its legal structure, its customs, uses, and collective beliefs, tendencies spontaneously agreeing with the common good. Such a society has achieved the highest kind of common liberty. It has reached a condition of genuine autonomy.

Our purpose is now to inquire about the way that authority can work for the achievement of liberty, or against it, both in man and in society.

Authority and Liberty

The history of the modern struggle for liberty is to quite a large extent made up of a rebellion against the imposition, upon the human mind, of any definite way of thinking. Modern liberalism is above all a claim for the freedom of thought. Accordingly it seems convenient to consider in the first place what authority may have to do with the knowledge of the truth.

The proper subject of truth is the act of judging. There, and there alone, the mind becomes aware of the relation of conformity existing between its own interior construction (the enunciation) and the reality of things. Enunciation, a synthesis of concepts, constitutes only the matter of a judgment; the formal element is the assent that the mind gives to the enunciation. As for the reason our assent is given to some enunciations and refused to others, it is quite clear that the evidence of the object, the evidence of the conformity between the enunciation and the real, is the only cause which can determine the assent without hurting in any way the natural aspirations of the intellect. Perfect knowledge, that is, scientific knowledge, proceeds from self-evident principles and extends their evidence to enunciations not immediately evident. So long as those perfect conditions of the knowledge of the truth are preserved, the uttering of the assent is neither a matter of liberty nor a matter of authority. The object is sovereign and wholly causes the determination of the mind. In the presence of an evident object the mind has its assent forced upon itself and does not enjoy any kind of liberty; withdrawing one's attention (closing one's eyes) is the only way to escape the recognition of a fully enlightened truth.[9] Nor has authority anything to do with the issuance of the assent in evident matters, since authority can only be exercised upon a subject endowed with some kind of liberty.

Now a great number of truths do not appear under those conditions of perfect enlightenment. Moreover, owing to the progressive character of the human mind, many truths which are intrinsically capable of evidence are not perceived as evident by the mind in the first phases of its development; their evidence will even remain permanently beyond the reach of many individual intellects. The beginner in the sciences can not perceive at once the evidence of scientific demonstrations. True, many years will pass before

[9] See John of St. Thomas, *Cursus Philosophicus, Ars Logica* II, 24, 3 (Marietti ed. p. 762).

the most fundamental demonstrations will have become evident to him. What about the condition of scientific truth in his mind during those years of painstaking expectation? Experience shows that unless a firm assent is given to truths whose evidence is not yet perceived there is a good chance that their evidence will never be perceived at all. This is why the beginner in the sciences, so long as he is not able to see the truth, and in order to become able to see it some day, must provisionally believe in the trustworthiness of a teacher. The authority of the teacher provisionally substitutes for the evidence of the object. Moreover, the notion of beginner does not apply only to schoolboys. All of us remain beginners in many respects throughout our lives. The most learned treatise of science contains relatively few statements that are fully evident to the author: around this nucleus of personal scientific certitude is organized a huge complex of statements which are simply believed on the authority of other minds.

This need for an authoritative help in matters that are objectively demonstrable is particularly felt in the field of metaphysical and moral truths. Those are truths of the greatest significance for human salvation; on the other hand their evident recognition is so particularly difficult that it can in fact be realized only in a small number of privileged cases. But that is not all, for the most precious truths, those which are most directly relevant to the salvation of man, are the secrets of God entrusted to Holy Church, of which nobody can have here below an evident perception. Here as elsewhere the intervention of authority to determine the theoretical judgment is but substitutional: faith substitutes here below for the promised vision and disappears when the mysteries of the divine life become evident to the beatified soul.

From all these considerations it results that the functions

of authority, so far as the theoretical order is concerned, are extremely important although they can never be more than *substitutional*. The liberal revolt against authority in that order represents possibly a sincere tribute to the ideal of objective determination which is that of theoretical knowledge. It represents also a proud refusal to recognize that the possession of truth is for the human mind a slow, progressive, and always precarious achievement. Most of all it represents a monstrous spurning of the most invaluable gift that the divine generosity could make to man, the revelation of the secrets of the divine life.

Turning now to the functions exercised by authority in the practical order,[10] we should say that some of them are still of a substitutional character. To be governed by someone else may be expedient on the ground of one's inability to govern oneself. This inability may be entirely normal and natural, as in children, or abnormal, as in the feeble-minded and the criminal. Here again the function with which we are dealing refers to an extensive object: all men are unable to achieve a complete self-government for about a third of their life, and many of them will be exposed to dreadful mishaps throughout their lives unless they are given some kind of guidance, in the pursuit of their own proper good by people whose reason is more highly developed.

[10] Beginning with this paragraph Prof. Simon summarizes his position on the nature of authority. The text generally follows the line of argument taken in his volume, *Nature and Functions of Authority* (Milwaukee: Marquette Univ. Press, 1940). These ideas on authority were subsequently developed in his *Democratic Philosophy of Government* (Chicago: Univ. of Chicago Press, 1950) and in *A General Theory of Authority* (Notre Dame: Univ. of Notre Dame Press, 1962). The statement on authority in this text has been retained in order to maintain the continuity of the argument and, more importantly, because Simon in this text more clearly relates his theory of authority to freedom than in other places. (Editor's note.)

It must be emphasized, however, that this function of authority, being made necessary on the basis of some deficiency, disappears when the best conditions of rational and virtuous practice are realized. The supreme question is whether authority has still some function to exercise under ideal conditions or, what amounts to the same thing, whether authority has any essential function. Considering a society made up only of reasonable and virtuous adults,[11] we wonder whether it is necessary for such a community to be submitted to some authority. Those who would answer in the negative have not understood the nature of common action. The common action of rational beings implies their common adherence to a common rule of action, to a practical judgment which has to be *one*, if there is to be any common action at all. How can the adherence of a plurality of minds to a single practical judgment be steadily assured? We are here very far from the conditions proper to scientific judgment, which, on the basis of the universality, necessity and evidence of its object, is *de jure* capable of causing a unanimous agreement of all minds. In matters relevant to concrete practice, unanimity is not only precarious, it is also thoroughly casual. Since action takes place in the midst of inexhaustible contingencies and implies an anticipation of the future which can be at best only probable, nobody can show with full evidence what is the best possible course of action for the group in pursuit of some common good. To take homely examples, how could it be made evident that this family should spend their summer vacation at the seashore rather than in the mountains? How could it be made evident that it is better to move right now than to stay another year in the old home? Yet, if all

[11] This is not a utopian fiction: there is no reason why a very small community, for instance, that composed of a man and his wife, should not include only reasonable and virtuous people.

minds composing the group do not assent to the same practical judgment, the unity of action is destroyed and the obtaining of the common good made impossible. For lack of any steady principle of unanimity the only way to assure unity of action is for all to submit to one practical judgment. This is the essential function of authority: to assure the unity of action of a plurality of men in the pursuit of their common good.

Besides its substitutional and its essential functions, authority still enjoys a function which should properly be called *perfective*. Assuming that a community is made up of people fully capable of self-government in the pursuit of their personal good; assuming that their unity of action in the pursuit of their common good is assured by proper authority, it is still expedient that those who are less gifted —less intelligent, less experienced, less strong-willed, less virtuous—be guided by those who possess a more eminent degree of reason, will power and virtue. This guidance is not utterly indispensable as is that exercised over the child; it is not as cogently needed as the power of unifying society in its common action. It is not absolutely indispensable to the *esse* of the particular good or to that of the common good, but it is necessary to their *bene esse*. As a matter of fact, the psychology of those who are intelligently submitted to an intelligent leadership shows that the good leader is not only appreciated for his ability to unify the society in a course of action which is thought to be the best possible, but also for the propulsion received from him toward better forms of life. In the happy event that the members of a society love their leader and feel proud of him, it can even be surmised that their predominant feeling toward him is the realization that under him everyone becomes better—professionally, socially, morally, humanly.[12]

[12] Considering the condition which would have been that of man-

So far as the *forms* of authority are concerned, we have to deal in the first place with the Aristotelian distinction between the *despotic regime* and the *political regime*. A regime is said to be despotic when the subjects are not endowed with any power of resistance; it is said to be political when the subjects are legally endowed with some power of resisting the orders they receive. It is to be noted that the Aristotelian notion of political regime is wider than that of a democratic check on the possible abuses of authority. The power of resistance can take the form of a democratic control, it can also take the form of a legal status unconnected with the democratic principle.

The opposition between the dominion of freedom and the dominion of servitude has quite a different meaning. Whereas despotic and political regimes are defined from the point of view of efficient causality, the opposition between the dominion of servitude and the dominion of freedom proceeds from the point of view of final causality. Considering the power of the head of a society as a principle of action, we recognize that this power may either be limited by some power of counteraction or not be limited by any such counter-power. Considering, on the other hand, the purpose for which people are ruled, the final cause of their being ruled, we recognize that this final cause can lie either

---

kind if man had not sinned, St. Thomas states that men would have been submitted to government for two reasons: "Primo quia homo naturaliter est animal sociale. Unde homines in statu innocentiae socialiter vixissent. Socialis autem vita multorum esse non posset, nisi aliquis praesideret, qui ad bonum commune intenderet. Multi enim per se intendunt ad multa, unus vero ad unum (Essential function of authority). . . . Secundo, quia si unus homo habuisset super alios supereminentiam scientiae et justiciae, inconveniens fuisset, nisi hoc exequeretur in utilitatem aliorum." (*Sum. Theol.* 1a, q. 96, a. 4.) In the preceding article, St. Thomas has shown that in the state of original innocence there would have been many inequalities among men, without there being any defect or sin in the less gifted ones.

in their own good, or in the common good of the society, or in the private good of the ruler. [One who is ruled for his own good or for the common good is a free man, one who is ruled for the private good of his ruler is a slave.] We thus have a notion of servitude which is both very wide and accurate. Whenever the power of a man over another man is used for the private good of the former, the latter is in a condition of servitude, however free he may be to choose his trade, his residence, etc.

Finally, mention should be made of the instruments of authority, persuasion, and coercion. Persuasion is a moral process through which a person generates a disposition in the free will of another person. Coercion is a physical process causing involuntariness in the person submitted to it. Authority cannot be in any way identified with coercion, which is only one of its possible instruments. As a matter of fact, persuasion is used by authority much more often than coercion. No social life would be possible if authority should have all its decisions enforced by coercive procedures.

This short survey of the functions, forms, and instruments of authority should enable us to discuss the question of the relationship between authority and liberty. It is understood that we shall not consider liberty empirically with its imperfections but rationally as an absolute perfection whose progress implies the getting rid of its imperfections.

There is not, *de jure,* any opposition between authority considered in its essential function and the progress of liberty. The essential function of authority, viz. assuring the unity of action of the multitude in the pursuit of the common good, is a thing good without qualification whose necessity plainly derives from the nature of society. Yet, even the essential functions of authority have often been attacked on the ground of a philosophy of liberty. In order to realize the implications of a philosophy which carries that far the struggle against authority, nothing more is needed than an elementary understanding of the notion of common good. Let us not say that the common good is an end which *is* intended by a group of people: the common good is an end of such a nature that it *has to be* intended in common and achieved through common action. Whoever opposes some principle indispensably required for common action is bound to brush aside the very notion of common good. Now a liberty that revolts against the common good has most decidedly fallen away from its adherence to the end, which is the primary condition of its perfection. The individualistic revolt against the requirements of the common good turns to a state of lonesomeness, indecision, that witnesses the triumph of the forces of disintegration within the person himself and ends logically in a state of solipsistic despair.

Now it may well happen that by accident and because of a misconception of the common good, a sharp conflict arises between the requirements of liberty and the demands of an authority engaged in the pursuit of a misconceived common good. There is an obvious misconception of the common good whenever that which is really evil is proposed as a good to the common action of a society; but the common good can be misconceived under much more subtle conditions. There is a misconception, a perversion of the common good merely if an end which could be satisfactorily achieved through the initiative of the individual or through that of a small social unit is forcibly incorporated into the end to be pursued directly through the action of a larger social unit. The principle of authority must be regularly supplemented by the principle of autonomy.[13]

[13] In a booklet entitled *Nature and Functions of Authority* (Milwaukee: Marquette University Press, 1940), I have given these principles the following formulas: Principle of Authority. *Wherever*

The relationship between liberty and the perfective functions of authority can be treated briefly. It seems exceedingly plain that the influence of a wiser superior can only liberate the freedom of the inferior from its possible irresolution and from the dangers of choosing wrongly. But the direction of the superior will not remain really perfective unless the idea of authority, here also, is supplemented by that of autonomy; for if the superior, by providing the inferior with ready-made decisions, deprives him of the opportunity to exercise his own judgment, the influence of the superior becomes detrimental and certainly impairs the progress of liberty. In its perfective functions more than elsewhere, authority has to act mildly if it is to complete its tasks. Perfective authority usually gives its pronouncements the form of advice and counsel rather than that of binding precepts.

Quite different is the case when authority substitutionally provides for the proper good of a person or that of a minor society. Here, the need for authoritative guidance results from a deficiency, a privation. Inasmuch as liberty is founded on the superdetermination, the superactuality, the supersufficiency of a cause, it is plain that the reason which makes authority necessary is the same as the reason which makes the full possession of liberty impossible. Insofar as the liberty of the subject grows, i.e. insofar as his ability to choose without failing to reach his end and asserts itself, his need for being governed decreases. The increase of liberty means the decrease of authority. The perfect achievement

---

the welfare of a community requires a common action, the unity of that common action must be assured by the higher organs of that community. Principle of Autonomy. Wherever a task can be satisfactorily achieved by the initiative of the individual or that of small social units, the fulfillment of that task must be left to the initiative of the individual or to that of small social units.

of liberty implies the complete doing away with the substitutional functions of authority.

Any failure to understand the meaning of this conflict inevitably gives birth either to a destructive revolt on the side of the inferior, or to no less destructive abuses on the side of the superior. So long as the inferior really needs to be governed, that is, so long as he is really unable to direct himself toward his proper good, freedom from authority means exposure to a greater risk of missing his ends. On the other hand, if authority goes too far in any way, it fails to train the inferior in the proper use of liberty and postpones indefinitely the day when self-government can be achieved. The best authority is that which can disappear from its substitutional domain without its disappearance being noticed.

We have already noticed that among the functions of authority that liberal spirit most objects to that which is concerned with theoretical questions. Even if he concedes that authority has some essential function in the practical order, a liberal would feel reluctant to recognize that it has anything to do with the knowledge of the truth. The psychological causes of that attitude must be carefully analysed. It may happen that a liberal be a thorough agnostic, a sceptic, or a pragmatist: the authoritative protection of the truth seems to him a nonsensical idea, since he thinks that truth is beyond the reach of the human mind. It may happen also that a liberal be neither a pragmatist nor a sceptic, but only an optimist, a sincere lover of truth who takes it for granted than an unlimited freedom of thought, expression and discussion will necessarily result in the greater advantage of truth. Similarly, the liberal assumes that the greatest possible liberty of individuals in economic relations will necessarily foster the best possible forms of production and the most equitable ways of distribution. The question is what accounts for that necessary prevalence of the better either in the intellectual order or in the economic order. Can it not be objected that in an uncontrolled competition, error may very well prevail over truth and iniquity over justice? The way that liberal economists speak of such entities as *nature, the natural order, Providence*, shows that they surreptitiously imagine, within the stream of economic relations, a benevolent genius, an *invisible hand*, a reliable spirit, whose inconspicuous intervention directs chance occurrences and contingencies toward the greatest possible welfare of the *homo oeconomicus*. This fiction destroys the reality of chance and contingency. The disappointment experienced by those who had put their confidence in an uncontrolled freedom of economic transactions exemplifies the hard realization that the world in which we are living is not only a world of reason and legality, but also a world of chance, where evil may very well occur *ut in pluribus* unless it is held in check by the labor of human reason. Just as evil can prevail in economic relations if chance occurrences and inordinate drives are left uncontrolled, so error in the minds of men. This justifies the endeavor made by societies to provide truth with some kind of protection and privilege.

As to the form that this protection should assume, let us say that it has to be determined by prudential considerations in reference to each particular case. We are well aware that merely if the protection given to the truth is obsolete in form, it may well hurt truth rather than protect it. Abstracting from this problem of modalities, we have to consider whether the intervention of authority in theoretical matters essentially conflicts with the progress of liberty.

Here the supreme principle is that the determination of the theoretical intellect under ideal circumstances, as we already noticed, is neither a matter of authority nor a matter of liberty, but a matter of objectivity. Now, few people enjoy the privilege of having the most important truths of the natural order disclosed to their minds in such a way as to have their minds thoroughly determined by those truths. Even for those few people, the complete disclosure of the truth takes place only after a long period of research. Moreover, the possession of the truth by the human mind always remains precarious and no one can assert that the truth which appears to him in full evidence today will not be veiled by some interfering illusion tomorrow. For the great number of men who will never reach an evident perception of metaphysical and moral truth, for the privileged one also during the long period of the search for truth, and even for those privileged ones after they have achieved an always precarious conquest of truth, some authoritative protection against the forces of error is salutary in every way. This protection does not conflict at all with liberty, since liberty, let us repeat once more, is a power of choosing the proper means to the right end, which power is thoroughly impaired by any failure to intend the end properly. Is it not evident that the right intention of the end depends primarily on knowledge of the truth? Any theoretical error concerning the great metaphysical and moral truths radically corrupts the source from which right action springs. The right intention of the end and the domination over the means are born of the knowledge of the truth. *Veritas liberabit vos.*

If truths capable of evidence need some authoritative protection against the powers of error, this holds a fortiori for the great number of truths which are not, under ordinary conditions, capable of complete enlightenment. In the field of ethics there are, besides principles which can be demonstrated, a number of secondary principles of the greatest importance for the welfare of man and of societies which do not seem to be capable of demonstration. They

are the object of an act of belief partly determined by the
intervention of free will. Here, as elsewhere, any guarantee
against the risk of a wrong choice is purely advantageous
to freedom as such. Woe to a society that permits the collective beliefs upon which its ethos rests to be called arbitrarily into question! Finally, there are the revealed truths which
cannot become evident to anybody in this world. The
adherence of the mind to those truths is most properly a
matter of authority and a matter of liberty, since the assent
of faith is commanded by free will (moved by divine grace)
under the authority of God and His Church. Rejecting
the revealed truth is the most disastrous use that man can
make of his freedom since such a rejection makes him blind
to the very principles of his salvation and diverts him from
the ultimate end of human life.

Turning now to the forms of authority, we can state briefly
that the despotic regime and the dominion of servitude conflict sharply with the progress of liberty. Both must decrease
if liberty is to increase. However, they do not conflict with
liberty in the same manner nor to the same degree. Nothing
prevents, at least *de jure*, people from being despotically
governed for their own good or for the common good, that is,
not as slaves, but as free men. It may well occur that a despotic
regime be needed for the protection of a liberty which is
not yet sufficiently strengthened against the forces of evil.
The reasons which may justify a despotic regime are apparently analogous to those which justify the substitution of authority for self-government, and both cases can be discussed
in a similar way so far as the problem of liberty is concerned.
On the contrary, the dominion of servitude, the mastership
exercised by man over man for the private good of a master,
conflicts with liberty, even when it does not conflict absolutely with justice.

Finally, as to the instruments of authority, it is entirely
plain that the progress of liberty requires the use of per-

suasion rather than of coercion whenever coercive procedures can be safely abandoned. Whenever coercion must be
employed, the men in power should never forget that coercion fails to achieve its most elevated end, unless it fosters
the growth of virtuous dispositions which finally render coercion unnecessary. It is extremely striking to notice that, whereas
liberals most generally consider coercive procedures as good
only to insure external order, St. Thomas emphasizes the
pedagogical function of coercion: to prepare the way for virtue
by establishing a system of good habits that make easier the
triumph of the virtuous will over the passions.

Totalitarianism and Liberty

To return to the historical consideration which appeared
as the starting point of this study, it seems fitting to attempt an interpretation of the "authoritarian" crisis which is
today devastating the world. However anxious we may be
not to overrate the part played by ideological factors in the
revolutions of societies, it is unquestionable that the development of modern totalitarianism is linked to a general dis-
affection toward liberalism and a general feeling that more
authority is needed in all forms of social life. The whole
point is whether the criticism of liberalism and the search
for a restoration of authoritative principles have been rightly
conducted.

The preceding discussion has sufficiently shown that we
consider liberalism as a dreadful error, and that we are not
inclined to make any concession to what constitutes the
heart of the liberal philosophy, i.e. the illusion that a
boundless competition of atomic forces is likely to promote
all kinds of perfections, both in the individual and in society.
Now the most redoubtable errors are often associated with
the most precious truths, and it happens that partisans fight
an error on account of the truth with which it is associated

rather than on account of its intrinsic wrongness. Up to now, the main results of the crusade against liberalism have been a scornful disregard for justice, blacklists, indiscriminate proscriptions, and mass slaughters.

Whoever has observed with any degree of sociological insight the development of the totalitarian movement knows that the enemies of democratic liberties, despite their noisy worship of authority and discipline, are really animated by the worst spirit of anarchy—a spirit of revolt linked to a spirit of group imperialism. This remark refers not only to the plebeians who have led the totalitarian revolution, but also to a good number of conservatives, who gave their plebeian allies such efficacious support in the struggle for the "New Order." The general revival of interest in the philosophy of Nietzsche can be taken as a symbol of the anarchic and imperialistic spirit which so successfully concealed itself under a claim for order, discipline, authority, etc.

Now that the totalitarian movement has reached its climax, its true character can best be evidenced by a comparison between its actual achievements and the purposes for which authority stands. Whereas authority has the duty to preserve the reign of Truth in the minds of men, the totalitarian state has established its power, and keeps itself in power, through a cynically avowed technique of lying. Whereas authority has the duty to perfect people by having them subjected to the influence of the best ones, the totalitarian movement has brought into power thieves, murderers, and traitors. Whereas authority has the duty to promote the autonomy of minor societies, the totalitarian state, materializing a dream of Rousseau, has achieved an unprecedented extermination of societies within the state, going so far as to dissolve associations of chess-players and stamp-collectors. Totalitarianism has effected a systematic destruction of legal protections, installing everywhere arbitrariness and a ruthless despotism in place of the guarantees of the political regime. Above all, totalitarianism has diverted authority from its essential function by substituting the private interests of a group of self-appointed leaders for the common good of society as the main object of politics. Just as the origin of the totalitarian regime is best accounted for by the identification of one party with the whole of the state, so its aim is best accounted for by the subservience of the whole of the state—*to say nothing of the enslaved countries* —to the ambitions of the party in power.

The history of the last twenty years and particularly of recent developments shows that the victory of totalitarianism has been made possible only by the betrayal of conservative groups, foolishly blinded by their group hatreds to the real character of the totalitarian movement. It can be wondered whether the consciousness of those groups, whose historical mission was to preserve the right sense of authority and to keep a balance with the social forces especially devoted to the promotion of liberty, will ever be reawakened. The least that can be said is that, for having made themselves, in so many cases, the treacherous go-betweens who delivered their countries to the "plebeians-in-chief," traditional conservatives have impaired for a long while their ability to represent the principles of order and authority.

If this is true, the men and the groups which are, by historical tradition, dedicated to the defense and promotion of liberty, will have to assume the defense and promotion of the true philosophy of authority, deprived of its traditional supporters by the collapse of the old conservatism. From those who have inherited the spirit of freedom of the English, American, and French Revolutions, a great ideological purification is demanded. They are now expected to rid themselves of the last remnants of the liberal sophistication and dedicate their lives to the undivided cause of liberty and authority.

3

Freedom
and Community

THE PROBLEM OF HUMAN LIBERTY appears in three main relations, namely, to natural causality, to divine power and to
the power of human communities. Some remarks on the first
two issues may help to define the subject of this chapter,
which is human freedom in the context of human community.*

* The notes appended to this and the following two chapters
consist of annotations from the manuscript papers of Professor Simon
on "Freedom and Community," "Autonomy and Authority," and
on "Political Society." Where Professor Simon's notes indicated
that he had intended to amplify his remarks or make reference to individual authors, the suggestions he proposed have either been written
into the text or given in the notes.
Similarly, the materials drawn from the notes of Professor Vukan
Kuic have been incorporated into the notes or put into the text; in
the latter case, the use of his notes is indicated where relevant.

When freedom is considered in relation to natural causality, the latter appears first of all as a restricting principle and as an obstacle. According to many interpreters, natural causality makes freedom impossible. It does more than restrict it: it causes it to be but an illusion. Yet the history of the question shows that what appears first as an obstacle and is regarded by some as a cause of impossibility is regarded by others as the very principle and cause of liberty.[1]

In the relation of human freedom to divine power, there arises the suggestion of an obstacle and a conflict. Many theories endeavor to preserve human freedom while describing it as in conflict with divine power.[2] These theories suggest

[1] Professor Simon in his lectures on "Liberty and Community" at the University of Chicago during the spring of 1955 made the following brief comments on natural causality as a restrictive principle. These comments were taken from Professor Vukan Kuic's notes.
"*a*. Epicurean philosophy denied Democritus' determinism of atoms and contended that they deviate, swerve ceaselessly, free of necessity; this denial of a natural philosophy was intended to safeguard human freedom.
"*b*. Under whatever concept it is disguised some men regard God as an obstacle to human freedom. An illuminating example from pagan philosophy is the classical concept of fate versus freedom, epitomized in the tragedy of Oedipus.
"*c*. Social obstacles to individual freedom have always been obvious and empirical. The relevant question here is whether society sometimes enhances freedom.
"It should be pointed out that some philosophers have taken all three obstacles to freedom—or any combination of them—as aids rather than obstacles."
For a further analysis of freedom and causality see Chapter VII of Yves Simon's *Traité du libre arbitre* (Liège: Science et Lettres, 1951), pp. 93–112.
[2] With respect to the relationship of human freedom to divine power. Professor Simon wrote the name "Hartshorne" in the margin. Charles Hartshorne's *The Divine Relativity* (New Haven: Yale University Press, New Edition 1964), contains the following passage (pp. 141–142) which touches the subject of Professor Simon's concern:
"Since an object always influences, but cannot dictate, the awareness of itself, we influence God by our experiences but do not

that there is something in human freedom which escapes the power of God, which in other words is safeguarded by being kept away from the power of God. Other theories hold that the power of God actually rules out the possibility of freedom. Such words as freedom and liberty are still used, but the thing that they designate is no longer freedom from neces-

---

thereby deprive him of freedom in his response to us. This divine response, becoming our object, by the same principle in turn influences us, but here, too, without removing all freedom. The radical difference between God and us implies that our influence upon him is slight, while his influence upon us is predominant. We are an absolutely inessential (but no inconsequential) object for him; he is the essential object for us. Hence God can set narrow limits to our freedom; for the more important the object to the subject, the more important is its effect upon the range of possible responses. Thus God can rule the world and order it, setting optimal limits for our free action, by presenting himself as essential object, so characterized as to weigh the possibilities of response in the desired respect. This divine method of world control is called 'persuasion' by Whitehead and is one of the greatest of all metaphysical discoveries, largely to be credited to Whitehead himself. He, perhaps the first of all, came to the clear realization that it is by molding himself that God molds us, by presenting at each moment a partly new ideal or order of preference which our unselfconscious awareness takes as object, and thus renders influential upon our entire activity. The total or concrete divine mover is self-moved, as Plato correctly said. Only he who changes himself can control the changes in us by inspiring us with novel ideals for novel occasions. We take our cues for this moment by seeing, that is, feeling, what God as of this moment desiderates.

"The foregoing account challenges comparison with the traditional view, which merely says that God creates out of nothing, and that his rule of the world is essentially the same as this creation. Scarcely the faintest glimmer of insight from experience seems to shine through such language. Our knowledge that objects influence but do not coerce subjects is left entirely unexploited. Is this the way to attain even the slight comprehension we are capable of— to pay no attention to the one mode of influence we in some degree understand?"

Professor Charles Hartshorne taught philosophy at the University of Chicago. Professor Simon and he were acquainted and exchanged views on philosophical matters.

sity, which, by the terms of these theories, has disappeared into the all-embracing and universally necessitating power of God. However, in the case of the relation to God as well as in the case of the relation to nature, what is interpreted by some as an insuperable obstacle is interpreted by others as a principle and a cause. In the school of St. Thomas Aquinas, every part, phase, and aspect of a free act proceeds from divine power. The modality by reason of which the free act is free is no less certainly caused by God than any other aspect of any act or thing. If human freedom had to be taken away from the range of divine causality, then it would disappear into nothingness, for lack of being created. The same divine perfection that some metaphysics endeavor to safeguard at the high cost of human liberty finds, in the metaphysics of St. Thomas, a glorious assertion of its excellence in the creation and maintenance of freedom of man and other rational creatures.

The conflict between freedom and community is a commonplace in romanticism. Ever since Rousseau, the search for freedom in the wilderness has been a favorite escape for personalities ill-adjusted to social circumstances. In some cases, liberation is expected of solitude itself; more commonly, the solitary wanderer is looking for a company more dependable than that of men, and he leaves the human community only to enter into a community of natural energies which, while being personified, retain their natural innocence.

The images ordinarily associated with the idea of liberty have been described by Chateaubriand with a rare happiness of expression.[3] When arriving in Philadelphia, this disciple

[3] The excerpt from Chateaubriand and Professor Simon's comments are the present editor's translation of the opening paragraphs of Yves Simon's Traité du libre arbitre, ibid., pp. 9–10.

The first quotation in the text comes from Chateaubriand, Voyage en Amérique, Œuvres Complètes (Paris: Pantheon Litteraire, 1837), t. II, pp. 21–34.

of Rousseau was surprised not to find among his hosts "the rigidity of early Roman customs" such as he ascribed to the ancient world. But in the virgin forest he was certain to find or rediscover what he had come to look for: "primitive liberty, I have rediscovered you at last. I go as the bird who flies before me, who is directed only by chance and who is hindered only by his own choice of shadows."

People boast of loving liberty and hardly anyone has a right idea about it. When, in my trips among the Indians of Canada, I would leave the homes of Europeans and find myself for the first time alone in the midst of an ocean of forests, having, so to speak, the whole of nature prostrate at my feet, a strange revolution occurred in my soul. In the kind of delirium that seized me, I followed no road; I went from tree to tree and indifferently from right to left, saying to myself: No more roads to follow, no more towns, no more cramped houses, no more presidents, republics, kings, especially no more laws and no more men. Some men? Yes. Some good savages who do not get in my way nor I in theirs; who, as I, also run freely wherever the thought leads them, eat when they will, sleep where and when it pleases them. And to attempt at last to reestablish myself in my original rights, I will devote myself to a thousand willful acts which will enrage the Dutchman who serves me as a guide and who in his soul believes me to be a fool.[4]

Men of the twentieth century may agree with the Dutch guide. However, who of us would dare to pretend that he has always rejected the authenticity of the conception of liberty that Chateaubriand described with the lovely sincerity of his young romanticism? Is it not the current opinion that freedom is opposed to order? From that point on, the pace of the dialogue is fatally determined. For spirits fascinated by the idea of order, liberty can only be the object of received concessions. Confronted by them, the lover of freedom makes out,

[4] The second quotation is from Chateaubriand, *Essai historique sur les révolutions*, II partie, Ch. 57, *Œuvres Complètes*, t. I, p. 206.

with a certain success, that an excess of order destroys life. So on one side or the other liberty finds itself assimilated to a disorderly, exuberant, and luxurious life, an inventive and creative, inspired and foolish life. It gives color and warmth to everything. But the world disappears in chaos. They admit that disorder or a tendency to produce disorder is of the essence of freedom.[5]

[The cause of the urge to find freedom away from human society is obvious: at every instant, our choices are restricted by laws and regulations, by customs and by prejudice. However, just as it is impossible to dismiss without examination the theory that human freedom is ultimately grounded in natural necessity, so it is impossible to dismiss without examination the theory that human freedom, which is restricted in many ways by the requirements of community life—an obvious, but perhaps a superficial fact—is also, in another sense, caused and promoted by human communities.]

Alienation versus Integration

We propose to begin this inquiry into freedom in relation to community with a study of slavery,[6] servitude, and related situations.

[5] *Traité du libre arbitre, ibid.,* p. 10.

[6] A number of books on slavery have made their appearance or have been reprinted in the last several years in the United States, probably reflecting a growing interest in the Negro question. The first three entries listed below relate to slavery in the United States. The fourth book by David Davis deals with a broad perspective of slavery in world history.

a. Elizabeth Dongan, *Documents Illustrative of the History of the Slave Trade to America,* 4 vols. (New York: Octagon, 1965; originally published in 1933).

b. Susan Dabney Smedes, *Memories of a Southern Planter,* edited by Fletcher M. Green (New York: Knopf, 1965).

c. Eugene D. Genovese, *The Political Economy of Slavery* (New York: Pantheon, 1965).

The slave exists outside of the community; in him the privation of freedom coincides with a privation of community life. Apparently, it is the same factor which deprives him of his share of human freedom and of his place in the human community. No doubt, much can be learned from the connection of these privations. In contrast with the picture of freedom sought in the wilderness, slavery suggests a relation of interdependence between liberty and community.[7]

Servitude admits of many forms and degrees. We propose to describe those that are distinguished by their philosophic significance:

1. In the most extreme case, the state of servitude involves complete denial of human rights and the assimilation of the subjected person to a thing whose maintenance makes no sense save insofar as it serves the interest of the master.

---

d. David Brion Davis, *The Problem of Slavery in Western Culture* (Ithaca, N.Y.: Cornell University Press, 1966).

[7] Professor Kuic's notes reflect additional views of Professor Simon on the subject of slavery:

"In American slavery polemics John Calhoun defended slavery as an everlasting need of society—good even in a democracy—and supported his thesis by quotations from Aristotle.

"The story of slavery in America is tailor-made for the Marxian interpretation of history: the invention of the cotton gin which required cheap labor increased the demand for cotton; the institution of slavery which was tacitly assumed to be dying out from the time of the Declaration of Independence, was suddenly revived and defended by ideology, that is, by a pseudo-philosophy professed and advocated by a group in a moment of history; it contains elements of truth, pragmatic, sociological and evolutionistic.

"There is, of course, true philosophy motivated by the search for truth, but the philosopher is everlastingly tempted to indulge in ideology. Thus in Aristotle, there is a series of subjects treated as ideology, i.e., by reason of his social and historical position; these are especially and almost exclusively slavery and labor."

For additional insights into slavery by Professor Simon see his *The Tradition of Natural Law*, edited by Vukan Kuic (New York: Fordham University Press, 1965), pp. 8, 17, 29–30.

2. In a less extreme case, the human rights of the slave are recognized, but the master still claims strict ownership of the slave's labor. Generally, such appropriation of labor entails the permanence and hereditariness of the slave's condition. Accordingly, the institution of slavery plays a decisive part in the division of society into groups defined by status.

3. Without questioning human rights or ownership of the human labor force, there still is servitude, if not slavery, whenever a subjected person is governed for the sake of a good which is neither his nor that of the community, but that of a master. Such seems to be the most essential feature of servitude.

St. Thomas has discussed the question whether, in the state of original innocence, man would have exercised dominion over man. He saw an essential difference between a dominion aimed at the good of the governed or at the common good, and a dominion aimed at the private good of the one who governs. In a community free from evil, dominion for the sake of the governed, as in the case of paternal authority, and dominion for the sake of the common good, as in political societies, retain their necessity and their excellence. But dominion exercised for the sake of the master is excluded; for, to be governed toward the good of another is painful. It is a dominion of servitude. Dominion aimed at the good of the governed or at the common good becomes free men. When the servant is directed toward the good of another, such alienation is painful. There is no alienation of the subject in a government exercised for his own sake. There is no alienation in being governed for the common good: the common good of our community is in no sense alien or foreign to me. But the dominion of servitude is a dominion of alienation. Servitude is essentially defined as a state of subjection involving the alienation of human effort.

A dominion involving such alienation can be described as a dominion of exploitation. However, the connotations of the word "exploitation" are so bad that such a word must be avoided in a discussion where problems of lawfulness ought to be examined. It would sound puzzling to ask whether the exploitation of man by man is ever legitimate. But the question of the legitimacy of servitude certainly ought to be considered; this question should be discussed in terms of alienation rather than in terms of exploitation.

Servitude

Let us now consider the most typical vindications of servitude. This inquiry will follow the division of servitude into three unequal forms, the first two of which alone deserve also to be called forms of slavery.

To vindicate the most extreme degree of slavery, which is characterized by an unqualified denial of human rights, it is necessary to assume, in some way or other, that the slave does not belong to the same species as the master, that he has but the appearance of the human species. Such paradoxes assume diverse forms to suit prevalent ideas. At the time when the Spanish conquerors indulged in a frenzy of enslavement, someone suggested that the natives of the Americas, being descended neither from Sem, nor from Japheth, nor from Cham, were really not human beings, and thus could be dominated like beasts and things inanimate, with a perfect conscience. In the century of evolutionistic biology, the same idea can be recognized in the statement so popular during the years of Nazi preponderance, that there is a greater distance between the highest and the lowest races of men than between the lowest races of men and the highest races of animals. If a Negro, or a Jew, or a Pole, is entitled to use a beast of burden and to kill it when its maintenance is no longer profitable, men of the upper race have a more certain right to dominate the despised races without any other law than that of their own interest.

However, from the fact that the law of the land fails to sanction, or inadequately sanctions, the human rights of the slave, it cannot be inferred with necessity that these rights are ignored. The silence of the law may merely mean that the problem is left to the jurisdiction of the family. The familiar modern notion of broadly developed political organizations and of households whose functions are reduced to a minimum, may render much human history unintelligible by failing to account for the fact that many functions later assumed by the state—either accidentally or as a result of maturation and normal growth—had been left by earlier societies to inferior units of public law or to altogether private communities such as the family. The judicatory power of the head of the family over wife and children does not necessarily mean that wife and children are not entitled to fair treatment. It may merely mean that the duty of assuring fair treatment to all members of the family is entrusted, not to an appointed magistrate but to the head of the family. Between the underdeveloped political society and the family there would be, in this respect, a relation similar to that of the national government to the state in a federal union. A miscarriage of justice in Massachusetts or any other state of the Union is no business of the federal government; this does not mean that the federal organization is indifferent to justice, it merely means that except in cases whose relevance for the federation is direct, the administration of justice is a function of particular states. True, a state of affairs which allows private communities to use unrestricted coercion and to apply the death penalty bears the mark of primitiveness and social immaturity. It is not by accident that the administration of justice whenever serious measures of coercion are involved, belongs to the political society—whether state or federal union. It is by accident that issues involving serious forms of coercion are settled within the household; but such accidents may be frequent, and to ignore them would make much human history unintelligible. Down to modern times, circumstances which made it actually possible for political societies to discharge all the duties which normally are theirs have been, on the whole, exceptional.

In the more moderate forms of slavery, which still involve the strict appropriation of human labor, it is generally alleged that the arrangement is beneficial to the slave. Aristotle, who makes a decisive use of this argument, confesses, however, that the master remains the main beneficiary. If this were not the case, if the arrangement between master and slave were equally profitable to the master and to the slave, the dominion would be aimed at a common good and, in the words of St. Thomas, it would no longer be a dominion of servitude.

In innumerable instances the discussion of slavery has been confused by failure to see the difference between paternal government and dominion of exploitation.[8] The former

---

[8] In his manuscript Professor Simon noted that in the Spanish system of encomiendas the exploitation of the slave was described as the reward of the caretaker. This attitude toward slavery is another historical example of the confusion between paternal government and exploitation.

"The encomiendas," say Louis Bertrand and Sir Charles Petrie in their *History of Spain* (New York: Macmillan, 1952), pp. 185–186, 198, "reduced the Indians to slavery. The concession of an estate or district was officially obtained, together with all of the natives in it, but always on the condition of converting them to the Christian faith. The Spanish colonists had the same titles as the emperor and king; titles of proprietorship and rights of sovereignty were legitimatized only by an apostolate. There was here—as we must admit—a very lofty and noble idea, which it was, unfortunately, only too easy to distort and falsify in practice. The colonists mocked at their apostolic duties, made a convenience of Christian charity

does not involve the latter, except by accident. The guidance exercised over children does not involve the subjection of the child to the interest of his parents. True, paternal government outside of the relation of father to son may also have the character of a service calling for a compensation. If the compensation is equal to the service there is no exploitation; if it is greater than the service, it calls for an explanation not supplied by the notion of a reward for the services of paternal government.

Considering, finally, servitude broadly understood as covering any situations in which, independently of the rigors of slavery, man is so subjected to man as to work not for himself but for another, the commonly proposed justification is derived from an aristocratic vision of society. In this perspective the noblest forms of human life are said to be unattainable without an unequal exchange between a relatively small number of privileged persons and the rest of mankind. Leisure is needed for politics, for knowledge, for art, for good manners and all forms of culture. Except in economic abundance, it seems that a universal law of equal exchange would subject all to drudgery, and, for lack of leisure and other facilities, the more noble forms of human life would disappear from society. Now the common good requires that the noble forms of life be represented in every society, even though a small number of men actually share in them. Inasmuch as the common good demands that the noble forms of life be represented in society, the means necessary to these forms of life are justified by the common good.

---

and refused to see in their Indians anything but slaves and beasts of burden from whom they extorted the utmost possible profit.

"Las Casas became the advocate and apologist of the oppressed Indians. He carried on a public debate hoping to obtain the royal assent to the abolition of the ecominciados. The supporters of the system tried to justify it on the ground that the natives were an inferior race."

At this point it is less relevant to pass judgment on the worth of this vindication than to consider its essential meaning. Since the state of servitude is defined as a subjection relative not to the common good, but to the private good of the master, it may be asked whether vindication by the requirements of the common good eliminates the essence of servitude. [There is certainly a considerable difference between being given orders for the service of the common good and being given orders for the service of a private person whose proficiency and accomplishments ultimately serve the common good.] In the latter case, the reference to the common good implies an indirectness of great psychological, moral, and social significance. The essence of servitude is not eliminated. But the conditions under which servitude can be vindicated are decisively affected by the theory that servitude is ultimately justified precisely by what it tends to deny, for example, the direction toward the common good. A vindication of servitude in terms of indirect relation to the common good suggests an aspiration to a state of affairs which would make that relation direct and do away with servitude.

Let us consider a task often accomplished under conditions of servitude and let us try to determine in what ways servitude can be suppressed without the fulfillment of the task being impaired. The division of labor in society often demands that a person should not spend time and energy on such jobs as cooking his food and sweeping his room. Such duties of domestic service have often been performed under conditions of servitude. [Our question is whether servitude necessarily follows upon the nature of the task, or whether it is just a contingent condition.]

It seems that servitude can be removed, without the nature of the task being changed, in three ways. Such a task as domestic service ceases to be exercised in conditions of servitude if it concerns a *public* person, considered precisely and exclusively in his public capacity. [Of two military men of equal rank one is assigned to the telephone switchboard and the other serves as orderly to the general. Running a switchboard in a camp is a duty of public character which, except by accident and plain abuse, does not involve laboring for the private good of another.] There is something personal about the assignment of an orderly, but the person whom the orderly serves is public, and it is by reason of his public character that the orderly is expected to serve him; when the commanding officer returns to private life, service for a public person is terminated.

If this description is correct, one way to put an end to servitude is to transform into public functions what used to be private tasks, and to change private persons into functionaries. This may account for some aspects of the connection between equalitarian ideas and the development of state socialism. The job being the same, the wage and the circumstances not being noticeably different, many people seem to feel, nonetheless, that whether the boss is a private employer or a functionary makes a great deal of difference. Indeed, so far as forms are concerned, it may make all the difference for it distinguishes a dominion of freedom from a dominion of servitude.

All other things remaining the same, such a task as domestic service loses the character of servitude when the wage of the servant is adequate to the service rendered. [The service goes to a private person and the servant takes orders from his employer; this subordinated position, coupled with the privateness of the employer would result in servitude if it were not for the restoration of equality by an adequate wage.] Again, servitude is defined as subjection to a master for the sake of his private good. The servant who receives adequate compensation is working for himself just as much as for his master. The psychological and sociological consequences of high wages are to a large extent traceable to the qualitative change brought about when the wage becomes equal to the service rendered. Here, as it often happens in human affairs, a quantitative change results in a change of quality. The relation of servitude disappears into a relation of equal exchange, and the supplier of such services as cleaning or cooking becomes a partner in a relation of exchange where he works for himself as much as for another person.

A difficulty seems to remain inasmuch as there is subjection and government. Let us compare for instance the case of a truck farmer who sells vegetables at a price equal to their value with that of a laborer who takes care of a vegetable garden for a wage equal to his work. The farmer enters into a purely contractual relation involving no subordination. The laborer subjects himself and takes orders. Does this state of subjection suffice to preserve the essence of servitude in spite of equality between service and wage? What is decisive here is that the division of labor may be equalitarian as between a tailor and a shoemaker, or not equalitarian as between a lawyer and a valet. When subjection is purely a consequence of the nature of the division of labor there is no servitude, unless the wage is unequal to the service.

The third method of doing away with alienation is the "servitude of love." Here, there is labor for the sake of another and perhaps subjection to his orders. Yet there is no alienation inasmuch as, through love, the other has become another self. It is of great importance to determine, no matter how roughly, the social significance of this way of ending exploitation. One thing is clear: whenever there is need for legally defined relations among men, love supplies no solution. It has been the mistake of utopian socialism to appeal to love when the problem required an answer formulable in legal or juridical terms and of such nature as to be enforceable by the sanctions of public powers.

Notice, however, that a factor of no use where there is need for legally defined and sanctioned relations may still be one of extreme importance. In many cases social progress is achieved by the substitution of legal formulas for dependence on benevolence. All that pertains to love seems to convey a risk of arbitrariness. Human arbitrariness is, of all the forms of chance, the least tolerable. No wonder if the effort to exclude arbitrariness develops into a tendency toward universal legalization which ignores the role of love in society and particularly the ability of love so to transform relations from within as to suppress alienation in countless instances where no other method is conceivable. In the tragedy of Claudel, *The Hostage,* one character exclaims "The revolution was not made against the king or against the nobles or against God, it was made against chance." Elsewhere another character complains that from now on "there will be nothing gratuitous among men." [9] Indeed, the systematic suppression of servitude either through the transformation of the person served into a public person or through the establishment of compensations strictly equal to the service rendered would restrict the domain of gratuitous action.

Here we touch upon one of the least known aspects of the theory of the family in Proudhon. His constant opposition to the romantic exaltation of love and his effort to promote, in the relations of man and woman, a spirit of self-control, dignity and justice may conceal the fact that Proudhon reserves to the family the energies that he refuses to use as principles in economic and political society. In a passage of *Justice* he discusses domestic service as follows: "You will have no servants except your wife, your daughter, your old mother, or a friend who likes to live with you. Your cook,

[9] Paul Claudel, *The Hostage,* translated by Pierre Chavannas (New Haven: Yale University Press, 1917), pp. 87 and 132. Professor Simon used his own translation of the text. The sense of his translation is reflected in the Yale version.

your seamstress, will be artisans with whom you will make contracts on a footing of equality." Thus we have two systems of relations in domestic life; one is entirely contractual and exclusive of servitude, the other is not equalitarian, it is not contractual, it rests on devotion—Proudhon did not like to use the word love. Domestic life for him is the place where the servitude of love plays its indispensable part.

But outside the family circle, the servitude of love has its part to play—the relief of misery is an obvious case, probably not the only one. It would be good to succeed in dividing clearly the fields of social life into those where the thing desirable is the highest degree among legal institutions and those where the thing desirable is the most extensive intervention of love. No doubt, the pole of the latter field is in family life. Precisely where should we place the pole of the system of legal relations? Is it in the state and in the relations of legal and distributive justice, or is it in economic life and in the relations of commutative justice? Something significant may be derived here from the connection, in Proudhon, of the juridical and the equalitarian concern. Perhaps it is in exchanges that justice is most completely independent of love. Justice is certainly not independent of love in the case of legal or general justice, which is obviously animated by love. Distributive justice, also, is animated by love. Indeed, it looks as though commutative justice, inasmuch as it simply does not involve a relation of love, constitutes the pole of the juridical system.[10]

[10] Professor Simon uses the word "juridical" in this paragraph to relate solely to the functions of the state when it judges in matters of contractual relations only. Juridical or quasi-juridical decisions in governments of course deal with a much wider range of concerns. They exercise responsibilities with respect to "legal, general or distributive justice" as well as "commutative justice."

It will be noted that Professor Simon has employed the language of Aristotle with respect to justice. Modern discussions of justice, spoken of by Aristotle as "legal, general or distributive," are most

Exploitation versus Integration

So far we have been considering alienation in relations involving authority and subjection. We now propose to consider alienation in relations which do not involve, at least not initially, directly, and formally, authority and subjection. I say "at least not initially, directly and formally," for we are going to see that alienation in processes of exchange often entails a distinct type of domination. The question whether alienation in exchange tends to cause a distinct type of subjection is worth examining. The general construction of an analysis of "exploitation versus integration" would be as follows: 1) alienation in unequal exchange, 2) domination resulting from such alienation, and 3) servitude to the community, defined as service to a false and illusory common good. No doubt, to be directed toward a false common good always involves some sort of servitude, but a case of particular relevance is the case in which the common good is false by reason of its not including the maintenance and promotion of freedom in the members of the community.[11]

We first consider alienation outside of relationships of subordination and subjection—that is, in the relationship of exchange and more particularly in the purely contractual rela-

---

often referred to as "social justice." Pope Paul VI has established an International Committee on Peace and Social Justice. The role of love in the development of both peace and social justice is clearly indicated by the remarks of Professor Simon.

[11] Professor Simon's manuscript at this point contains an extended analysis of usury, which has been omitted from this text. He analyzed usury (an inequality in exchange) as a form of alienation. Among other things he wrote, "The problem of usury is entirely distinct from the problem of the morality of incomes without the contribution of labor." His views on commerce and just price are elaborated in his *Philosophy of Democratic Government* (Chicago: University of Chicago Press, 1951), pp. 234–53.

tions of buying and selling. When commerce is philosophically considered, it of course includes space and time utilities. Classical economics stresses the law of supply and demand. Even where there is no sophistication of the market by reason of spreading false news through monopolies, etc., the oscillation of prices takes place. Even in an unsophisticated market the rule is to buy cheap and sell dear! A merchant may make each sale perfectly honestly, but in the end his wealth will be gained by a one-way exchange: from society to the merchant, never vice versa. [The general standard for merchant, farmer, and industrialist remains the common good; if there is no contribution to that good "wealth leaks out of society" and there is alienation. Social devices to stop the leaks are several: price fixing, organization of labor (indirect), cooperatives,[12] syndicalism, state intervention, especially in the form of taxation.]

Against the privation of liberty and the lack of integration in the community there have been two revolutions: a democratic one in the eighteenth century and a social revolution in the nineteenth. The first was against exploitation by way of subjection but it neglected the increasing extent of relationships of exchange. Let us take the unmistakable example of the bourgeoisie, the owners of the means of production, and the proletariat, the worker who has his labor for sale. The ensuing class struggle tends to be relaxed through the introduction of social legislation, but will persist as long as labor is a commodity on the free market. The laborer in modern society is a free agent, but his freedom is not supported by property. The modern laborer is free to sell the only thing he owns—his labor force; so he enters into an exchange with an employer.

[12] The paragraphs beginning on page 80 with "We first consider alienation . . ." through to the end of the chapter have been excerpted from Professor Kuic's notes on "Liberty and Community."

[The purpose of social legislation is to prevent human labor from being treated as a commodity in the market where the worker is at a disadvantage.] He can be replaced and cannot wait while the employer can wait or employ someone else. They are therefore not equal partners in exchange. Wages in a free market will generally be kept at a low level, i.e., at the cost of the worker's maintenance—the subsistence level. Such a system acquires a hereditary character and thus becomes a class system. In an order recognized by public law the members have a defined function toward the common good of society. A class relationship is different—it is marked by a tendency to secede from society. (Marx noted this tendency.)

The cause of the tendency to secession lies in the fact that the connection between the worker (proletariat) and society is a contractual one when it occurs in the market place. A labor contract of that kind does not found a community; it is and remains a mere partnership because of the fungibility of the laborer's good. A fungible good is replaceable by units of the same kind, e.g., in a sheaf of wheat, one unit is as good as another. On the contrary, works of art are not fungible because individuality matters and prevails in time. [A proletarian is typically fungible and because of his fungibility he is not integrated into the community.]

Social mobility in a society, however, makes for a different situation. In the United States where there is a high standard of living and the status of the proletarian is essentially voluntary, his activity is conceived of as a division of labor in relation to management, and a division of function. Thus the status of the proletarian becomes similar to a system of orders in which there is the same common good for one community. In Europe and elsewhere the situation is different. The proletarian's separation from society is expressed in the internationalization of the labor movement.

Bertrand Russell in *Freedom Versus Organization* describes, among other things, the exploitation of children in England. Does this mean that the bourgeoisie is vicious? Not necessarily: it is a logical consequence of labor being treated as a commodity and therefore coming under the laws of the market. The poverty of workers in Germany was greatly improved before World War I, but the situation was resented by them and remained explosive. The class struggle continued although, according to Bernstein, socialism was reformist rather than revolutionary.

Why did this happen? It was because labor continued to be governed by outsiders. It resented heteronomous government. It was for a similar reason that the Poles resented the Germans and the Irish resented the British. The bourgeoisie aped the aristocracy and tried to take over the paternalistic form of the latter under the system of orders. Such an effort only intensified the struggle because the situation is no longer the same. Society is now governed by class relationships and not by orders.

In socialist states it is not exploitation but a new managerial class which derives material benefits from its position that is of predominant importance. What is significant is that under socialism the individual working for the community is placed in a state of servitude through a perversion of the common good.

What is this corruption of the common good? The freedom of the members of a community is a part of the common good which must be constantly redistributed since this good is not separate from the community, that is, its members. Servitude in a socialist state thus places the proletarian in the service of a false common good.

4

Autonomy
and Authority

PERSONS IN AUTHORITY ARE ALWAYS TEMPTED to do more than
they are supposed to do. This is noticeable in the rule of
children, in the government of the family, and above all in
the government of political society. Thus one of the main
concerns of political wisdom is to establish checks and balances. Every authority is expected to trespass the proper
borderline of its action, to encroach on domains that are not
its own, to invade fields where it is not supposed to intervene,
and to monopolize functions which should remain distrib-
uted. For the sake of brevity, we shall refer to this tendency
as the imperialistic tendency of authority.

In order to describe with greater precision the meaning of
this tendency, it is necessary to refer to the basic princi-

ples of the theory of authority. As shown elsewhere,[1] the problem of authority can be stated in the following terms. We call *substitutional* any functions exercised by authority on account of the inability of deficient persons or societies to achieve self-government. The problem is whether all functions of authority are substitutional, whether authority whenever necessary is made necessary by deficiencies, or whether some functions of authority are grounded in the nature of society independently of any evil or deficiency. The problem is, in other words, whether authority, besides its substitutional functions, has any essential functions. As soon as this question is posed with clarity, the necessity of an answer in the affirmative is plain. The more obvious of the essential functions of authority concerns the unity of common action. By the very fact that a plurality of agents is involved, the unity of common action cannot be taken for granted: it has to be caused. Common action can be unified either by unanimity or by authority. The problem boils down to whether unanimity is a steady principle of united action. Clearly, a community made of ideally enlightened and well intentioned persons would be unanimous whenever there is only one way to the common good. But it often happens that the way to the common good is not uniquely determined, that the common good can be obtained in either of several ways and that, accordingly, neither enlightenment nor "good" will rule out a diversity of preferences. And yet common action has to follow an undivided way, or failure is certain. Causing unity of action when there is no foundation for unanimity is an essential function of authority. This function is relative to means. But it is in relation to the ends of common life, that authority exercises the most essential of its functions, which

[1] For a fuller study of Professor Simon's philosophy of authority see his *A General Theory of Authority* (Notre Dame, Ind.: Notre Dame University Press, 1962).

is the volition and intention of the common good materially considered.[2] It is not necessary to consider here the most essential function of authority, whose accurate description involves great difficulties. All that is required for our present purpose is a clear understanding of the division of the functions of authority into the essential and the substitutional ones.

The Imperialistic Tendency of Authority

It is now possible to describe with greater precision the imperialist tendency of authority. In the case of the substitutional function, authority succumbs to its imperialistic temptation whenever it fails to let the governed exercise all the self-government that he is capable of in every phase of his development. The meaning of imperialism is more difficult to describe in the case of essential authority. The essential functions of authority are distinguished by a direct relation to the common good as common. (I say "as common" in opposition to "as jeopardized by antisocial appetites or any other socially relevant deficiency.") From this it follows that these functions are contained within the limits of common pursuits, common achievements and common enjoyments. Notice that "common" is understood here in opposition to particular, not in opposition to individual. A community may contains several communities, which in turn may contain a diversity of communities of lower level. The common pursuits and achievements to which we are referring pertain to each community not only in opposition to the pursuits and achievements of an individual character, but also to those which pertain to the communities of the lower level.

[2] On the distinction between volition and intention of the common good see *Philosophy of Democratic Government, ibid.,* pp. 36–71 and A *General Theory of Authority, ibid.,* p. 52.

Tracing the borderline between what is the concern of the community and what is the concern of its parts is likely to be difficult in most concrete cases. The last word will belong, in each concrete case, to prudence (and one of the desirable effects of a system of checks and balances is to insure the proper consideration of the pros and cons in the deliberation). In a household the idiosyncrasies of everyone may be considered purely particular issues. Yet beyond a certain measure, these idiosyncrasies may harm the community. The difficulty of determining, in each concrete case, the proper measure, is only one aspect of the fundamental difficulty inherent in all that pertains to an operation in a system of contingency. What is philosophically relevant is to understand the proper natures and causes of the tendencies which operate with remarkable regularity in the midst of such contingent occurrences.

Let us, then, consider the factors by which the men in authority are inclined to overgovern; in other words, to decide by authority on a certain level matters which really pertain to other levels of decision. Of these factors the best known are the meanest. They certainly are extremely important, but their obviousness is such that no elaborate treatment is needed. Pride finds satisfaction in the exercise of authority, and a greater exercise of authority procures additional gratification of proud feelings. Since every ruler has been a subject, and since the experience of subjection generally involves some mortification, the exercise of authority is often experienced as a sort of revenge, and thus is made frantic by resentment.[3] Various forms of cruelty also find satisfaction in the exercise of power, especially when it involves the crushing of obstacles. All this is clear, and there is no question of minimizing the significance of these factors of mean charac-

[3] Professor Simon's manuscript indicated that he had Max Scheler's views on resentment in mind

ter. However, such factors owe the best of their power to their association with factors of loftier character, whose understanding requires careful analysis.

First of all, let us call attention to the fascinating beauty of order, regularity, and efficiency. When the question is whether a desirable state of affairs is to be brought about by the initiative of the most central, the most common and the best unified authority, or whether it should be expected to result from a multiplicity of initiatives, order and efficiency generally seem to lie on the side of the more centralized system. Experience shows that this may be a deceptive appearance, but deceptive or not the appearance is strong, and the line of the least resistance leads to the sort of order that centralization brings about. An order of a pluralistic description may be more valuable, more profound, and it may be more of an order, but it is hidden in the stream of contingent occurrences where it finds its realization and is devoid of glamour. To apprehend its beauty requires loftier powers of perception. The reason why spectacles such as military parades have a powerful appeal is that, through the strong centralization of the principle of order, they disclose the beauty of order in an easily accessible form. A community of farmers, each of whom manages his farm and his work autonomously, may be considered a wonderfully ordered thing, but its order does not strike the eye as does that of an army on parade. Such a community may surpass in productive efficiency any collective farm of the same size, but it is easier to be impressed by the efficiency of a successful collective farm than by the silent efficiency of a plurality of autonomous efforts.

There has been one period in the recorded history of mankind when the narrow restriction of government powers was commonly considered a thing obviously desirable. Let us call this period the golden age of liberalism. The uncertain date of its beginning and its end vary according to the countries considered; so far as Great Britain and France are concerned, the most characteristic part of this period coincides with the reign of Louis Philippe and the youth of Queen Victoria. In North America such characteristic years could be placed anywhere in a period beginning much earlier and ending much later. During that period, prevailing ideologies recommended that the domain of government be cut down to a minimum and foresaw that such reduction would actually take place as a result of the inescapable and normal development of society. Should it be said that during this golden age of liberalism the prestige of order has declined? True, the liberal age offers many expressions of a romantic attitude which sets in opposition order and life and exalts life at the expense of order. But these emotional expressions had much less to do with the course of political events than the vision of society embodied in the received systems of economics. All these systems recommended, in varying degree of inflexibility, that the government not intervene in economic life, and expected the greatest good to the greatest number to come from the free play of economic atoms. Strikingly, this vision is not related to the exaltation of life at the expense of order which is found in romantic authors of the same period. The economists believe that the world of free and unrestricted competition is a most orderly thing. Recall the "invisible hand" of Adam Smith, the providence of Frédéric Bastiat, and the benevolent nature which all trust with the power to bring about the natural order in society provided that human governments refrain from interfering. These appeals to providence, to nature and to the invisible hand signify that the economists do not believe that a world of non-regulated initiatives is delivered to chance. [Their mythology places the principle of order—providence, nature, invisible hand—inside the stream of the events that no human government or prudence has planned out or organized.⟩ By this mythological operation, chance is radically eliminated. Their idea is that the free play of economic relations guarantees an order which is the very expression of nature and whose splendor outshines any order planned by man. It is remarkable that the only period in which the men in power show a disposition to hold, in accordance with the prevailing ideas, that government should be kept within the narrowest limits, is precisely the time when there obtains a belief in the spontaneous realization of order. True, the liberal age offers exceptional examples of restraint on the part of governments. It is reasonable to relate this restraint to the prevalence of an ideology which deprived government of the prestige that it generally derives from its ability to effect miracles of order by attributing to ungoverned social nature the power of producing miracles of order with which no man-made order can compete.

The appeal of order and efficiency as a factor of imperialism possesses a unique significance in the technological age. At this point, it is relevant to recall that the influence of the technical environment upon human events does not take place only in the order of material causality but also in the order of exemplary causality. The main evidence of exemplary cause in this age is a belief in necessary progress caused and maintained by constant improvements in industrial techniques. When we consider that a certain state of techniques rules out or opens up such possibilities as an abundant agricultural production, or the fast transportation of large amounts of supplies over great distances, we are referring to a system of material causality. The habit of designating as a materialist interpretation of history any interpretation of social events in terms of technical environment causes a disposition to ignore the influence that the technical environment may exercise through the ideas, the models, and the pat-

terns or exemplars that it places in the minds of men. [Today
more than ever, the technical environment fills human minds
with images of irresistible efficiency and infallible regularity.]
In this connection the situation of mankind at the middle of
the twentieth century is widely different from what it was
but one generation earlier. Not so long ago, the common experience with machines included a large amount of failure.
Machines, in spite of their ability to work miracles, were
famous for their aptitude to get out of order; a comparatively
high ratio of failure in their operation served to recall that
the world born of human science is, like nature itself, a
world of contingency.

The feeling that human industry can outdo nature in perfection is an old idea. Helmholtz once said: "If an optician
had made an instrument for me as imperfect as the human
eye, I would have refused it." In the last generation the increase in the power of machines, and more generally of the
instruments placed by science at the disposal of man, has
been at least equaled by an increase in the regularity of their
operation. Philosophically speaking, whether a machine gets
out of order once a day or once a century makes no difference; a rare accident is an evidence of contingency as certainly as are frequent accidents. But when the issue concerns
the influence of physical experience on human visions and
attitudes the rarity or frequency of the accident may bring
about qualitatively different situations. We have reached a
phase in which the patterns resulting from the technical environment express a regularity hardly threatened by failure.
Still more significantly, our minds are dominated by the
image of a trend tending, at an ever-accelerated pace, toward
the limit of an absolutely faultless regularity. [In contrast with
these images of order, man appears as the only thing which
causes disorder and failure with appalling frequency.] Here is
a resistance to be crushed. The vision of unprecedented pos-

sibilities of order stimulates a new idealism which combines with misanthropy and a fierce feeling for the aristocratic distinction attaching to the possession of the principles of the new order. Among the features which distinguish the modern totalitarian state from the despotic and imperialistic enterprises of the past, the mark of the influence of the patterns supplied by technological regularity must be carefully considered. Emphasis is commonly laid on the possibilities placed in the hands of ruthless governments by the means of the technical age: quick communication, irresistible weapons, etc. The decisive fact may be the synergy of the material, the instrumental and the exemplary character of modern technology.

[In addition to the prestige of the social order, a factor of still greater profundity tending to the imperialistic use of authority may be the feeling of the quasi-divinity of society.] There is, of course, participation of everything (especially rational things) in the image of God. When Aristotle in the *Ethics* speaks of the "more divine" nature of the common good as compared to the private good, he uses the term "divine" in the Greek sense of uncorruptible, imperishable; he also has in mind the participation in divine attributes, i.e., the virtual immortality of society, its plenitude and its ability to perform (when its members act together) things almost superhuman.[4]

[The exaltation of society as a thing divine turns to an exaltation of what pertains to a social rule as a whole. If we begin with the idea that the goods of social life are incorruptible and of indefinite comprehensiveness, we are led to an idea of the quasi-providential presence of society and a sense of hopelessness of the individual faced by physical na-

[4] The full paragraph beginning with the phrase "In addition to the prestige of the social order . . ." was taken from Professor Kuic's notes.

ture.) But in spite of the individual's weakness, the wonders that society produces are in fact accomplished in and by individual members. Can society be described as a providence in its benevolent and protective arrangements of events? If so, how can governments be overthrown or attacked because of their failure to satisfy large segments of the community? What of the analogy with grace in its direction of personalities from within? Can government propaganda or coercion achieve such an effect?

Nonetheless, in countless daily instances society is what saves the human mind from doubt and desperation. We expect of society the creation of order in the intellectual aspects of social life. We expect of society a constant declaration of the rational. We are so convinced that what is rational must also be recognized and proclaimed by society that when social sanction is lacking, rationality is doubted. Thus, against the view that metaphysical propositions admit of demonstration, it is everlastingly objected that if such were the case some sort of consensus concerning these propositions would take place; from the absence of consensus the absence of demonstrativeness is inferred.

Notice the difference, in this connection, between metaphysics and other difficult disciplines. It has been said that only a dozen men were able to follow the most advanced theories of Einstein; it used to be said that only three men in the world could follow the last theorems of Henri Poincaré. However, society never left minds without guidance in the domains explored by Poincaré and Einstein. Society backed them, certified that they were reliable witnesses. How can society certify the testimony of witnesses who can communicate with only a few other individuals? In such a difficult discipline as physics, there is a concatenation of testimonies which finally reaches the common man and fills him with confidence. The vanguard scientist communicates his most advanced theories to extremely few, but those few communicate with a larger group of experts, and the latter with still larger groups and so on down to common people. Also, in such a difficult discipline as physics, not everything is hard to communicate. Parts that can be easily communicated constitute a guarantee which is extended to the parts which in fact admit only of extremely restricted communication. In metaphysics, on the contrary, there is hardly any part easy to communicate. The discrepancy between essential and factual communicability is by no means particular to metaphysics; it appears conspicuously in physics and mathematics. The great difference is that in physics or mathematics, society can do a great deal to reduce the discrepancy—or perhaps more exactly to correct its consequences—which it cannot do in metaphysics. How then are we to explain this difference between social possibilities in physics and in metaphysics? The obvious answer is that in physics experts are agreed, to a large extent, at all levels of expertness, whereas in metaphysics the experts themselves are divided. But this is still a shortsighted approach. The question remains whether metaphysicians of different views are all genuine experts or whether some of them are only seeming ones. Here the crucial point is to establish what we mean when we say of a metaphysician whom we consider wrong that he is, indeed, an able man, a man of great worth, a man of broad and profound knowledge, perhaps a man of genius? In metaphysics as well as in other domains, the qualities that we refer to when we say that a man is able, that he has a great worth, that his knowledge is broad and profound are recognized by society with sufficient regularity. The thing that society cannot do, in metaphysics and related domains, is to decide whether the doctrine proposed with ability, profundity and amplitude, expresses truth or error. It is precisely in relation to truth and error that the metaphysical expert is not regularly distinguished by society from the scientific expert. Society recognizes only the kind of expertness to which we refer when we speak of ability, profundity, amplitude, etc. It seems to have no criterion as to expertness regarding truth and consequently concludes that the experts are divided.

Freedom and Law

We now come to the relation of freedom and law.[5] Consider the common view that freedom is the power to choose between right and wrong. The right is not necessarily determined in unique fashion. According to the comparison familiar to Mr. Hartshorne, a poet is not restricted to writing a good or a bad poem: he has a choice among a diversity of good poems. [The relevant question is whether freedom of choice necessarily involves the possibility of making wrong choices, as the creativeness of the artist definitely involves the possibility of working against the rules of his art.] (The grammarian of Aristotle uses his grammatical art to make grammatical mistakes.)

The volition of the end contains the choice of the means. The wrong means does not lead to the end and is not really a means. However, the unqualifiedly wrong choice is that choice which takes the agent away from his ultimate end. The same means may actually lead to some nonultimate end. The problem is to see that the volition of the nonultimate

[5] While the central conception of this section on "Freedom and Law" is the same as that contained in the section on "Freedom and Autonomy" in Chapter II, the differences of approach are considerable. In Chapter II, Yves Simon indicated his agreement with Jacques Maritain, who had in *Freedom in the Modern World* propounded the distinction between freedom of choice and terminal freedom. In the present chapter Yves Simon has made an additional personal contribution to the understanding of the idea of "the interiorization of the law" and has freshly analyzed the relationship of "autonomy of free choice" with "autonomy in physical nature."

end is contained in the volition of the end which is ultimate. The perception of this relation is dulled by passions, habit, diversion, etc., hence the illusion that the power of choosing is in no way harmed, but by all means increased, by the possibility of making, besides good choices, a few wrong ones. When nothing conceals the fact that choice is contained in the volition of the end, it is entirely clear that the possibility of making a wrong choice, that is, the trouble, comes from the remoteness of the ultimate end.[6]

Thus, the process of moral improvement, by which the possibility of wrong choices is ruled out—though never in absolute and unqualified fashion—changes freedom of choice into itself, not into something else. This process consists of an interiorization of the law. One is not interested in freedom as autonomy unless he respects the law so deeply as to want it to get hold of his innermost self. In truth, there are two interpretations of autonomy, one characterized by emphasis on self which inevitably gives way to the spirit of arbitrariness. Another is characterized by such dedication to law that I do not want to be ruled by anything else than the law. I so hate arbitrariness, especially if I have anything to do with it, that I want my own self to be the abode of law and my own inclination strictly to coincide with the directions of the law. I can then speak of autonomy without sophistry. I have not erected my will into law, but the law has become the soul and form of my will. The interiorization of the law is then an operation involving much sacrifice. The rebel is unwilling to consent to such sacrifice because the law is something he does not care to have within himself. He finds it bad enough that the law hovers over him as a threat.

[6] Professor Simon's manuscript notation suggests that there be a study of "Choice and Happiness" which would endeavor to answer the question: "In what sense can happiness be said to be remote, although it is present at the core of all rational actions?"

[So long as the tendencies of a person are at variance with the law that he is bound to obey, the law remains, in varying degree, external to him.] The development of virtues is the gradual constitution of steady tendencies in strict coincidence with the law. Insofar as a man is genuinely virtuous, acts at variance with the law stir in him horror and aversion. Does this mean that their power of attraction has entirely disappeared? We know by experience that it often has not. The attraction familiar to the old self coexists with aversion in the new self born of virtue. The days of peace have not yet come. In the words of St. Paul, another law is felt, which wars against the Law. Autonomy is by no means unqualified: part of the self remains foreign to the law and the law remains external to it. [Yet in pain and struggle and exposure the just man can be said, in a proper sense, to be free from subjection to the law; insofar as love for what the law prescribes actually predominates in him, insofar as the rebellious law is actually kept under control, the just man no longer is placed under the law; rather he is one with the law by reason of victorious inclinations made of love for what the law demands and aversion to what it forbids.]

The meaning of autonomy in free choice and its excellence can be made clearer by a comparison with autonomy in physical nature. Every form of being involves a tendency to act, undergo, and react in a definite way. Because this tendency is really indistinct from the constitution of the thing, it is properly its own law, and things of nature enjoy autonomy in a proper sense. True, the autonomy of the things of nature does not entail absolute regularity of operation; yet operation according to law, in the sense of nature, is hampered by contingency alone: a minor factor of disorder in comparison with the initial condition of man, which is open to disorder not only by reason of contingency, but also by reason of ability to make wrong choices. Hence the feeling of contrast between the reliability of nature and the unreliability of man. [The solitary wanderer illustrated by early romanticism does not really mean to escape into solitude; as he steps out of the disappointing company of man, he means to join the company of beings more dependable and predictable in their behavior: trees that blossom every spring, and hazes and frosts faithful to their magic.] In this fidelity of nature, what man is actually seeking and admiring is a similitude, a reminder and perhaps a promise of his own state of affection. The difference is that in nature autonomy has the character of an initial fact, whereas in mankind it has the character of a terminal accomplishment, which indeed is never so total as not to call for new progress.

Vigny's poem *The Shepherd's Cabin* ends in aversion to nature because of its indifference to man. But this indifference follows upon the impossible fidelity that other poets treasured. With extreme appropriateness, aversion to the regularity of natural things is associated with a conversion to the unique, the perishable, the transient: *love what you never will see twice!* This desperate skeptical conversion to human affairs viewed in their becoming and impermanence expresses the defeat of a soul which no longer treasures the ideal of autonomy in free choice. To such a soul the inflexibility of nature appears as an insulting reminder of hopeless failure.

The interpretation of nature as a system of autonomy attained the highest degree of firmness and consistency in the philosophy of Aristotle. The hylomorphic theory means that in a universe of perishability and within the stream of universal becoming, things still have a way of being what they are and of acting according to what they are. In the metaphysically more complete vision of St. Thomas a nature is "a certain idea, viz., of the divine art, placed in things and by which things are moved toward their ends." Such views, very close to common experience, are opposed by powerful arguments and sentiments both in the philosophy of nature and in metaphysics. So far as metaphysics is concerned, opposition to the autonomy of natural things is rooted in a sentiment describable as follows. A vivid intuition of the perfections of the absolute engenders the sentiment that relative things ought to be denied those perfections.[7] The perfections under consideration are those which admit of unqualified, infinite, absolute realization, or at least are held to be such: reality, unity, beauty, glory, etc. An irresistible intuition says that these perfections belong to the absolute alone and that every good reason we may have to attribute them to things of our experience ultimately consists in an illusion. Indeed it is not possible to keep living and thinking if one denies with no subtlety or qualification that the things of our experience have reality, unity, beauty, etc. Because unqualified denial is factually impossible, the tendency to deny such perfections keeps the philosophic movement endlessly going.

After having considered the meaning of autonomy in the individual person, and in physical nature, let us consider it in society. Just as Aristotle throws light on diverse kinds of justice by describing the opposite diverse kinds of injustice, so we may learn much about autonomy in society by considering cases in which autonomy is felt to be lacking. Conflicts of nationalities supply many examples of resentment against rule by another. A dissatisfied national group does not always claim that the rule to which it is subjected is particularly unfair or unwise by reason of its content; no matter how wise the laws and decrees of the foreign ruler, they are hated and resented by reason of their being foreign. The

[7] Professor Simon's manuscript suggests at this point recalling the philosophical intuition of Bergson. For analysis of this intuition see H. Bergson, "Introduction à la Metaphysique," in *Revue de Métaphysique et de Morale*, January, 1903, and *L'Évolution créative* (Paris: Alcan, 1907).

feeling of being subjected to foreign rule constantly stirs the spirit of rebellion, as in conflicts of nationality and similar conflicts in colonial or ex-colonial areas.

A particularly significant case of heteronomy in the modern world is that of the proletariat. For a proletarian, to be ruled by bourgeoisie is to be ruled by outsiders, and against such a rule the normal reaction is rebellion. Toward the turn of the century a number of anarchist revolutionaries gave up their individualistic aloofness and joined unions. Anarcho-syndicalism holds or postulates that a sufficiently complete organization of the working men can take care of all the really important problems of society. The state disappears. The new organization is conceived as voluntary, equalitarian, nonauthoritarian. Anarcho-syndicalism made its appearance in France, Spain, in the United States as the I.W.W., and in the illusions of Samuel Gompers. There is, however, something behind the paradoxes of anarcho-syndicalism. These paradoxes, and what appear at first as crude illusions hardly expected of men who demonstrated great gifts for action, make sense if they are interpreted as expressions of an impassionate claim for self-government. In the mind of the revolutionary proletariat the notion of government was so closely connected with the experience of government by outsiders that the vision of an autonomic state of affairs seems to exclude all relations of authority and government. [What may look like sheer rebellion often boils down to opposition to foreign rule.] When the foreign character of the rule has disappeared, discipline and obedience often are no longer resented, as in the case of children who make up a republic of their own with strictly enforced rules.[8]

It is normal for every society to rule itself; precisely why

[8] Contrast this possibility with the anarchy of children's rule in the absence of strictly enforced rules as portrayed in William Golding, *Lord of the Flies* (New York: Putnam, 1959).

is this the case?—the more autonomous the rule, the closer it is to the matter to be ruled, the more effective it is. Here, as well as in the individual person, the perfection of autonomy is identical with perfect orderliness. Observance of the law is perfect when the law is so totally interiorized that there is no longer subjection to it. In what sense can it be said that there is no subjection in the case of a law which is that of our own group? There remains subjection of each to the law of the group, but insofar as the group is theirs, in other words, insofar as we as persons are members of their group, the law is our law and subjection has disappeared. The individual as such has the character of a part and the part is irreducibly subjected to the law of the whole; but because the person as such has the character of a whole, one may conceive, at the limit, a coincidence between the law of the person and the law of the group.

Freedom and Organization

We now come to the problem of the relation between freedom and organization. This can be described as the Saint-Simonian problem. According to the Saint-Simonists, history is made up of an alternance of *organic* and *critical* periods. The Greece of the early ages knew an organic period whose end was marked by the critique of Socrates. The Middle Ages were an organic period, followed by the Reformation and the Revolution—a long critical period. Saint-Simonism is the system of the new organic period. Liberty, especially by way of freedom of thought and expression, plays a historic part in the critical periods. It destroys obsolete institutions and beliefs, and this is a significant task. But when the time has come to build and to organize, liberty must yield to another principle. The celebrated formula of Engels, "substituting the administration of things for the government of persons," is essentially Saint-Simonian. Because of a constant emphasis on the end of the exploitation of man by man and on the association of men for the peaceful exploitation of nature, Saint-Simonism, especially in its early stages, has an engaging liberal appearance. In fact, what it rules out is only the domain of exploitation; so far as pursuits free from the stain of exploitation are concerned, it is one of the most authoritarian systems ever conceived and, in many respects, the pattern of the modern totalitarian state. The Saint-Simonian school soon grew into a church, and in a few years it was plainly declared that the actions of the faithful, down to the most particular, ought to be regulated by the priests.

Let us now consider the consequences of the excellence of autonomy so far as the relation between contract and community are concerned. Let us first describe briefly some fundamental types of social relations:

1. There are contractual relations unconnected with any lasting establishment, for instance, a sale and a purchase; 2. There are contractual relations of lasting character, as in the society called mere partnership; here a lasting society is founded by contract, and it remains a society of contractual character; 3. A contract may found a community which can be dissolved at will by cancellation of the contract; 4. A contract may found a community which can be dissolved by cancellation of the contract, though not at will but only in definite circumstances, and 5. A contract may found a community which can not be dissolved at all.

Insofar as contractual relations obtain among men, there is no government. Men bound by contracts alone are interdependent, but not subjected to each other. If all human relations could be built on the contractual pattern, authority would disappear. It is often said that the need for government results from the social nature of men; it should be said more precisely that government is necessary because human nature demands life in communities. If the associations necessary for human welfare were all of the contractual type, man would be a social being without being in need of any government.

We may now ask whether the excellence of autonomy demands that the domain of contractual relations be just as large as possible. To specify: plainly, there are cases in which the nature of the purpose demands a community organization and rules out the contractual method. If, for instance, the purposes are military, there is no alternative to the community called an army. But if the problem is farming, experience shows that a variety of methods may conceivably be used. Land may be divided into family-size farms. The family indeed is a community, but farming, under such a plan, is not a community business, or is one but on a small scale; it is primarily the business of individual initiatives coordinated by contractual relations. Legislation may be so devised as to perpetuate this state of affairs, as in the Napoleonic code, whose dispositions, in matters of inheritance, are designed to maintain the division of the land into small lots. The community principle plays a much larger part in aristocratic estates and in company-managed agricultural enterprises. Finally, farmland can be owned by the government and exploited directly by its services.

The tendency of liberalism, in the classical sense of this word, is definitely contractual. Most significant is the fact that when liberal dispositions are applied to the problems of the family, the community founded by the contract of marriage evolves toward a mere partnership, i.e., an association of a purely contractual character. From the old stages of an indissoluble community, marriage comes to assume the status of a community that can be dissolved under fixed and rare circumstances. The next step is that of a community dissoluble at will. In close connection with this movement, relative to the duration of the community founded by the contract of marriage, an internal evolution takes place, which brings about a gradual decrease of the relations of the community type and a gradual increase of partnership relations within the man-and-wife association. True, the tendency to bring about such transformation of the couple admits of degrees, and many liberals have been opposed to the more daring phases of the evolution just described, but these liberals are said to be conservative so far as marriage is concerned, which confirms the present interpretation of liberalism.

The first significant form of socialism, that is, Saint-Simonism, constitutes an extreme reaction in favor of community organization. As ground for this reaction let us mention first of all a search for rationality in the exploitation of physical nature. On the world scale on which it is envisaged, the exploitation of nature demands a maximum of strongly unified common action and community organization. Secondly, the trend toward extreme forms of community organization is fostered by a highly emotional sense of brotherhood in action and in distribution. Such a sense of brotherhood is harmed by the competitive individualism recommended by the classical economists.

The anarchism of Proudhon can be described to a considerable extent as a reaction against the community-mindedness, and the corresponding authoritarianism of the Saint-Simonists. The contractual anarchism of Proudhon attains its climax in his book on the *General Idea of the Revolution in the 19th Century*.[9] Here his declared purpose is the

---

[9] After his Diplôme d'Etudes Supérieures at the Sorbonne and in preparation for a doctorate, Yves Simon devoted several years to the study of P. J. Proudhon. All of this material is now in manuscript form at the Jacques Maritain Center, Library of Notre Dame University. See also Professor Simon's articles: "Le Problème de la Transcendance et le Défi de Proudhon," *Nova et Vetera* (Fribourg, Switzerland, 1934), pp. 225–338, "Notes sur le Fédéralisme Proud-

universal substitution of exchange for contribution and distribution, and of contract for authority. According to Proudhon's interpretation of human evolution, the lumping together of *order* and *government* is an accident pertaining to the youth of mankind. In the early stages of human evolution government is the only possible embodiment of order. Yet order is a genus and government is but one of its species. Order by subordination befits immature societies: the time has come for mankind to do away with authority and achieve a higher form of order, viz., an order by coordination.

The couple and the family are not included in this revolutionary change. The interpreters of Proudhon have often been puzzled by the contrast between his audacious contractualism in economic and civil relations and his strict maintenance of authority in the couple and in the family. Indeed, the evolution of the couple toward a purely contractual relation is altogether foreign to Proudhon. Most interpreters emphasize the contrast between his treatment of the family and his treatment of economic and civil societies. This contrast unquestionably signifies that Proudhon perceives a world of difference between the family and any other association. However, his unwillingness to make the slightest concession to the movement which tends to substitute contractual relations for community relations in the man-and-wife community may be said to contain a warning concerning the general character of Proudhon's contractualism. The man who is so little of a contractualist in his treatment of the couple and the family may well not be so much of a contractualist as he seems to be, in his treatment of economic and civil relations.

Beyond doubt, Proudhon is not, in the treatment of any

honnien," *Esprit*, n. 2 (Paris: April, 1937), pp. 53–65; "D'Aristote à Marx," *Revue de Philosophie*, N. S. Tome VII (Paris: Dec. 1938), pp. 71–78.

society, an individualist. This should be considered of decisive significance: when the question is whether Proudhon is or is not an individualist, the contrast between his attitude toward the family and his attitude toward other societies disappears altogether. All his work is permeated by a powerful sense of the reality and the worth of collective life. The understanding of collective life is for him the key to the problems of social science; the force of collectivity is for him the agent of justice, the energy whose orderly growth promises to bring one day the reign of justice. The strongest pages ever written against the atomistic dissolution of society in individualistic democracy have been written by Proudhon and are found in his *Solution of the Social Problem*. If the contractualism of Proudhon, in domains other than the family, is unqualified and successful, the contract principle must be able to effect the integration of the individual in society. If it does not, the contractualism of Proudhon, as expressed in the *General Idea of the Revolution in the 19th Century* fails at least in part. In fact, the final emphasis on federation rather than contract and the cautious restoration of the principle of authority suggest that Proudhon, in the complete maturity of his genius, had come to realize the insufficiency of the contract principle.

Gurvitch, the twentieth-century French sociologist, pursues a system of integration which may not be contractual but remains strictly equalitarian.[10] With the constant emphasis on integration, he systematically opposes the notion of authority, or what he actually understands by this term. The purpose being the integration of man in social wholes, the question is whether the contract, as such, does not bring about a whole. The contracting parties remain face to face.

---

[10] See George Gurvitch, *Sociology of Law* (London: Kegan Paul, 1947). Yves Simon reviewed this volume of Gurvitch for the *Review of Politics*, IV (July, 1942), pp. 361–412.

They have no common life and no common action. If this does not seem obvious in all cases, it is because of the multifarious combinations of contract and community which we have sketched in the foregoing.

Proudhon's reluctance to recognize the laws of community may be due to a large extent to misunderstandings concerning the basic meaning of authority. In Proudhon, and Gurvitch as well, authority is constantly identified with a dominion of exploitation. Moreover, to it, a character of transcendence is attributed which seems to involve the confused extension to all kinds of communities of features strictly proper to spiritual and supernatural society. One of the most faithful continuators of Proudhon, Edouard Berth, wrote that in the free workshop the leader would be interior to the group in the way in which an orchestra conductor is contained in the orchestra. This expression holds for every society except the one which is divine by its origin, its purpose, its inspiration, and its means of action. But, as known, the distinction between the temporal and the spiritual, with all its implications, appears extremely late in the consciousness of societies and often fails to attain satisfactory clarity. To conceive authority as transcendent in communities of a purely natural character is to attribute to it a character of externality in sharp conflict with the aspiration toward the state of autonomy. Let it be granted that any authority exterior to the group that it rules conflicts with the autonomy of the group and of its members. If authority is divine, its transcendence does not entail any character of exteriority, for God is more interior to me than I am to myself. But if transcendence is attributed to an altogether natural authority, as happens whenever a natural and temporal society is insufficiently distinguished from the spiritual society, transcendence means externality and violence, and authority enters into conflict with autonomy. In order to recognize without further inhibitions that integration is a property of community, all that is needed is to dismiss an arbitrary interpretation of authority in terms of transcendence.

We now have at hand the material needed to answer the question whether the excellence of autonomy demands that contract be preferred to community whenever the function to be performed admits of a merely contractual arrangement. Plainly, there is nothing in the contract as such which opposes the principle of autonomy. Persons engaged in a contractual relation are in no way subjected to government by another. So far as the contractual relation is concerned, they are free from rule by another person: to say it with greater force, they are free from foreign rule.

But one thing that the contract does not do is to contribute the ability to achieve self-government. This ability is the privilege of strongly constituted personalities, and so we are led to consider the part played by society in the constitution of personal strength. With an insight akin to the best intuitions of Proudhon, Edouard Berth writes: "The individual has never been great and strong; he has never been a personality except by the operation of forces which transcended the individual and raised him up to realities. When the individual was born a member of a family, of a trade, of a town, of a province, of a church, of organisms or institutions which produced mores and made up substantial realities, he was seized by collective forces, brought up by them, pulled out of animal subjectivism, raised up to the social and human level; he was able to become *a personality*: hence the strong and powerful individualities of which the Old Regime offered so many examples." Again, the reason why those things cannot be done by merely contractual relations is that a contract is not the constitution of a whole and cannot insure the life of a society within an individual.

Still another insufficiency of the contract is that it treats man not as a person but as a functional agent. Consider things strictly from the point of view of autonomy: autonomy demands personal, not only functional, development; if man is treated by society predominately and systematically as a functional agent, he is given no chance for development. The lack of personal development jeopardizes the autonomy of the group as well as that of the person.

It seems that the word "personalism" was coined by Renouvier. In spite of a strong emphasis on the notion of person, the word "personalism" remains foreign to the vocabulary of Proudhon. Daniel Halévy, in his early study on *The Youth of Proudhon* (1906) speaks of the "personalism" of Proudhon and remarks that it is unrelated to romantic revolt. Halévy was also a reader and admirer of Renouvier in the late twenties; he probably had read Renouvier much earlier and taken from him the word "personalism." Developments in diverse personalistic movements between the two world wars include Maritain's personalism in *Three Reformers* and subsequent studies; Mounier and his team, the New Order, Berdyaev, von Hildebrand, and before him, Scheler, the California journal *The Personalist*, etc. These movements are, to a large extent, independent of each other, and it would be altogether unreasonable to treat "personalism" as one doctrine. However, these several personalistic movements, which are apt to clash with each other on very important issues, have some aversions in common. For one thing, the personalistic movements are all opposed to the totalitarian state. Personalisms also seem to have in common an aversion to the mechanization of human life and even to the extensive use of machines. But this may be reducible to the functionalization described above. Secondly, they all evidence some sort of aversion to the old individualism.

Society and Contemplation

[We now turn to the question: is social life needed by the contemplative as a way to and preparation for contemplation, although such life is transcended by contemplation itself?] With respect to the utility of social life in its preparatory phase, the following points should be considered: (1) the need for a teacher as witness, and (2) the need for questioners and dialecticians. There is an analogy between the dialectical aspect of learning and the operation of the practical intellect called deliberation; in both cases a plurality of considerations is involved, which is best procured by a plurality of persons. It seems that teaching does not require plurality as essentially as the dialectical process. The solitary character of contemplation should be explained in terms of a contrast with the reasons why society is needed in the phase of learning. The contemplative is beyond the utility of the teacher as well as that of the dialecticians. Insofar as the actuality of contemplation is concerned, society would be merely a cause of distraction.

With regard to the right to lead a life of contemplation, I have used the expression "to secede into contemplation," but the propriety of the expression "to secede" raises an interesting problem. In spite of appearances, the contemplative may be so related to society as not to be seceding from it. We have to consider the common argument against the contemplative life: that the contemplative does not serve society; that he is a parasite. A vindication of the contemplative by some inconspicuous utility would not do. No matter how useful the contemplative may factually be, the essence of contemplative life is not usefulness, and a vindication in terms of utility would be a vindication in terms of accidents. In fact, in what ways can it be said that a contemplative is useful to society? (1) By his example. But if his example is useful, the life of which he sets an example is understood to be worth imitating. (2) The contemplative is useful by his teaching. But here there is a serious difficulty: the teaching of the contemplative may be considered useful in relation to contemplation itself and we are again confronted by the problem of the worth of contemplation considered in itself. His teaching of contemplation may be considered useful insofar as his contemplative activity is considered preparatory to further knowledge of a practical character. This is how many scientists apparently satisfied with a utilitarian vindication of science strongly defend the importance of disinterested research. If disinterested contemplation is worthy only by reason of its relation to applicable knowledge, then it no longer has the terminal character generally ascribed to it. More exactly, the primacy of immanent action entails the primacy of disinterested knowledge over applicable knowledge and, within the system of disinterested knowledge, the primacy of terminal action entails the primacy of contemplation over research.

Vindication in terms of utility is not the only kind of vindication. Indeed, it would make no sense if it were not understood to hold in relation to a vindication in terms of intrinsic excellence. In all orders, things excellent lie beyond utility, as for example, health beyond the means used to preserve it or to restore it. To ask about health the kind of questions that we ask about medicines and diets would make no sense. Likewise, contemplation does not have to be justified in relation to some further good to which it would be a way: it is itself the best life whose excellence ultimately justifies other ways of life. The contemplative is related to society as the fruit to the tree.

Is the contemplative then outside society? The contemplative belongs to society by the action that he takes in the order of final causality. Just as the mover by efficient causality is, in a very proper sense, present in what it moves, so there is a presence of the thing desired in whatever desires it. This supplies a new approach to the question: for it asks in what sense is the contemplative *good* for society? Again, his essential goodness does not consist in a relation of utility. The decisive insight may be this—to be useful is only one way of being "good for": the end is "good for" whatever strives toward it and is present in whatever strives toward it. Even if the contemplative, as soon as he has attained his state of accomplishment, should disappear into the wilderness and never be heard of again, he would remain present in society by the order that he causes in it in the capacity of final cause and intended fruit.

The motion of society by the contemplative and the beneficial presence of the contemplative in society can best be seen by contrasting the effects of diverse visions of life upon society. If the men who make up a community place ultimate happiness in the enjoyment of material goods, the whole system of relations constituting the formal part of society is marked by the character of these goods. Sensuous pleasures may be said to be present in all parts of a society dedicated to their pursuit. Likewise, military achievements are present in all parts of a society dedicated to warfare; examples are Sparta, the Cossacks, and bellicose Indian tribes. Another example, hard to manage but powerful if properly managed, would be that of a society dedicated to culture. Finally, if we try to find in history some material, no matter how incomplete, for a description of a society where an ideal of contemplation is cherished, Hinduism might supply the best material.

It is rarely said that it is the beneficial presence of the contemplative in society which will do most to explain a society dedicated to culture and to the perfection of minds.

But the fact could be substantiated. It would then be possible to show how the community procures the freedom of contemplation and how the freedom of the contemplative procures the order of the community.

Let us finally emphasize that in all the acts of common life, the most profound is communion in immanent actions. True, immanent acts of knowing the same truth, if exercised by solitary individuals with no awareness that the truth they know is also known by others, would be a collection of strictly individual acts, not a communion. But what was said in the foregoing of the solitary character of contemplative life does not entail individualistic isolation. A significant contrast can be drawn between solitude and individualistic isolation. Even if the contemplatives produced by a certain community were all scattered in strictly eremitical life, their common origins, their common roots would suffice to keep them within the community and to give their contemplation the character of a communion. The romantic solitary wanderer imitates the contemplative without having reached the proper phase of development. His case is much like that of the quietist who goes into passivity, an attitude proper to the latter phases of spiritual life, at a time when active modalities are still needed. When there is a premature withdrawal into solitude, behavior proper to a terminal condition in which the end is actually reached, is usurped by a person whose condition still has the character of being on the way. If the genuine contemplative causes order in society by reason of the final character of his condition, the solitary wanderer causes some sort of corresponding disorder. In contemplative hermits the community exercises its loftiest and most intense act of communion. Such acts do not need to be exercised directly by all members of a community; their loftiness and intensity are perhaps inversely proportional to the number of those who achieve genuine contemplation.

5

Political Society

WE PROPOSE TO USE SYNONYMOUSLY the expressions civil society, political society, state, and republic. We begin by asking whether political society is a distinct society, irreducible to any other type. In this statement of the question, we refer to the passage of the *Statesman* where Plato seems to hold that between a household and a state the main difference is one of size. This is opposed by Aristotle at the beginning of his *Politics*, where he says that the difference between the two is one of kind and that pressing the analogy would tend to destroy the state, i.e., that which is essential to the state. Plato's formula may well be essential to his whole theory of the unity of the state as he developed it in the *Republic*. But here again Aristotle maintains that making the state an individual, or as individual-like as possible, perverts the nature of political society.

De Bonald, in the traditionalist revolutionary movement in

the early part of the nineteenth century, also refused to differentiate between the family and political society.[1] His position, partly a reaction against rationalism and partly an obvious justification of monarchism, is that society is necessary and natural because it is essential to the production and conservation of men, and it is the family that is most essential to these functions. Political society, therefore, is rooted in the family. Subjects in every society proceed from the power of the society and its rulers as the child from its parents. Jacques de Monléon, in an analysis of de Bonald's theory of political society, says that the latter's argument would also mean that the family is the more perfect of the two societies.[2] In fact, what people like de Bonald say is not precisely that the state is reducible to the family; their contention is rather that the state is built after the pattern of the family and brought about by the same generating principle. As Plato and Aristotle have shown, the analogies between the family and the state do not hold unless we postulate a basic community of purpose and character for each of them.

There are also those who deny that the state should be shaped after the pattern of the family but hold that it should be shaped after the pattern of some other group. Proudhon (*Creation of Order in Mankind*) opposes de Bonald and says that the generating pattern of the state is supplied not by the family but by the workshop.

In the late eighteenth century a different but related movement developed with the birth of classical liberal economics: Smith, Malthus, Ricardo, Say, and, with qualifications, J. S. Mill. Its basic theory is that the state is a separate institution with well defined and limited functions.

[1] This paragraph includes relevant excerpts from Professor Kuic's notes on "Political Government."

[2] Jacques de Monléon, "Petites notes autour de la famille et de la cité," *Laval Théologique et Philosophique*, Vol. III (1947), pp. 265–66.

A century later this liberalism unconsciously approached anarchism in the state, which it defined as an organization to check evildoers and see to it that contracts are lived up to. The state tends to disappear as economic society is perfected. (Classical economics emphasized production and neglected consumption.) An outspoken representative of this school, although a minor figure, Charles Dunoyer, wrote: "The peak of perfection would be that everyone works and no one is governed." And "The best governed country would be the one where, common security no longer requiring a special and permanent force, the state would, so to say, disappear." [3]

There is a tenuous link between the theory of the state conceived as family and the latter type of classical economic theory in that in the two versions economics has traditionally been considered the proper concern of the family. Thus an economic society and a paternal society might have the family as a common element.

The socialist dogma of the withering away of the state was inherited from liberalism. Friedrich Engels summed up the common theory in the sentence: "The administration of things will replace the government of men." The real initiator of this tenet, however, was Saint-Simon or, better, the Saint-Simonists. Enfantin and Bazard wrote an exposition of the doctrine of Saint-Simon, a great work which became the source of later socialist theories of Marx, Engels, and others. [4]

The relevant problem is this: do the theorists of the

---

[3] Professor Simon wrote *Mémoire sur Charles Dunoyer* for his Diplôme d'Etudes Supérieures de Philosophie at the Sorbonne, in 1923. A copy of this manuscript was made available to me by Mr. Anthony Simon, son of Professor Simon. The sentences in the text were translated by Mrs. Paule Simon. They were by Yves Simon from an article by Dunoyer in *Le Censeur Européen*, an important liberal review published by Dunoyer and Charles Comte, Tome VII, 1818.

[4] See *The Doctrine of Saint-Simon: an Exposition; First Year, 1828–1829* (trans. George G. Iggers; Boston: Beacon Press, 1958).

withering away hold that the state should be shaped after the pattern of another group,[5] or do they hold that the state should, as far as possible, disappear? The answer is that both views are represented in these schools.

Coercion as Characteristic of Civil Society

It is of importance that we deal with the question of why civil societies are needed over and above other societies. In particular we must examine the theory of the state as an agency endowed with coercion.

It is commonly held that the power of coercion belongs to the definition of "state" and "government." By common opinion a society free from coercion would not be a political society or state and would not have a government no matter how much it might in other respects resemble what we are used to calling a state or a society directed by a government.

A first approach to the concept of coercion is supplied by contrasting it with the idea of voluntariness. Since voluntariness constitutes the most distinguished kind of spontaneity, coercion and voluntariness are strictly incompatible. A second approach to coercion contrasts coercion and persuasion. Coercion is exerted from without. Persuasion, on the other hand, while involving an influence from without is characterized by the fact that its influence is actively interiorized by the subject on whom it is exerted. When we say that a person has been talked into a certain way of thinking and acting by another person, we mean that the way proposed by the other person finally won the assent and consent of the first person who finally made it his own disposition. In persuasion the "from within" outweighs the "from without"

[5] Professor Simon does not discuss the constitution of the Church. His manuscript suggests checking "Taparelli d'Azeglio and inquire into theocracy, Caesaro-papism."

because the former is final, whereas the "from without" is initial.

Coercion admits of degrees inasmuch as the effect that it brings about may be traceable, in part, to a voluntary disposition. It often happens that the purposes of coercion are fostered by a concomitant and possibly related process of persuasion. One man held by several strong men determined to take him to a certain place may put up only a weak resistance because he is somehow persuaded that it is better to go along with them. He may be persuaded to go along for reasons independent of the threat of impending mistreatment or out of fear of what would follow his unwillingness to go along. In social relations the threat of coercion succeeds, in the overwhelming majority of cases, in bringing about the effects that would ensue from the actual use of coercion, if fear did not suffice. The expression "under duress" refers to the very frequent cases in which the threat of actual coercion motivates some sort of persuasion.

Clearly, when persuasion is motivated only by the fear of coercion, it ought to be described as a dependent of coercion, which thus admits of two unequal forms: according as it is actual or merely threatening. The case is quite different when the threat of coercion acts in association with an independent factor of persuasion. A taxpayer, for instance, may make an exact statement of income for no other reason than fear of fine and imprisonment. An example of the second case would be the case of a taxpayer who makes an exact statement both out of fear of punishment and out of reluctance to lie and to withhold from the state what belongs to the state.

Let actual coercion be placed at the left hand extremity of a horizontal line; persuasion motivated only by fear of actual coercion takes place next to it; farther to the right, persuasion born of the fear of coercion combines with persuasion born of some other motive, such as veracity and justice; still farther to the right there is persuasion unconnected with fear and unrelated to coercion.

The most familiar examples of coercion involve the use of physical force. However, not every method of influence is persuasive in character, and there is such a thing as psychical coercion. Its best known forms are hypnotic and posthypnotic suggestion. True, the power of the hypnotizer is not unlimited, and if his orders conflict badly with the subject's deep dispositions, they will not be carried out.[6] Let it be said, accordingly, that within the limits set by the deep dispositions of the subject, the hypnotizer exerts, through entirely psychological means, a power of coercion. Other famous examples of psychical coercion are found in mob phenomena. By general observation, a person caught in a frantic mob may act at variance with his principles, dispositions, habits, and all factors known to govern his ordinary behavior. Finally, a case of psychical coercion whose significance in modern society can hardly be exaggerated is intensive propaganda. Of course, no one can say where moderate propaganda comes to an end and intensive propaganda begins: this is what causes the worst trouble. Moderate propaganda is plainly aimed at persuasion; but when propaganda becomes intensive —a major factor of its intensity consists in its being unopposed—a qualitative change takes place without anyone being aware of it. The use of physical force is almost obsolete. The engineers of the soul have the situation well in hand. There is nothing metaphorical about their being called engineers, for like their colleagues in the factories and mines, they carry out designs through the controlled release of determinate causes. A social engineer, one of the cherished

[6] Professor Simon's manuscript cites William McDougall on hypnosis. A short analysis of hypnosis and its effects will be found in William McDougall, *The Energies of Man* (New York: Scribners, 1933), pp. 251–64

myths of scientific optimism, is a strictly contradictory concept so long as social processes remain the work of human spontaneity and freedom. But when freedom and spontaneity are stultified by propaganda, determinate causes bring about substitutes for social relations, and the destiny of men can be efficaciously engineered.

Considered in relation to authority, coercion has the character of an instrument. Coercion is what renders the presence of authority most noticeable. This is obviously the reason why authority is constantly confused with coercion, as if the essence of authority disappeared as soon as coercive procedures are excluded. Coercive procedures are the most unmistakable language that authority can speak to the imagination. Confusing coercion with authority is an accident traceable to a failure to transcend the data of imagination. However, when coercion is absent, authority lacks its primary and most direct way of addressing imagination. Then, other ways of addressing imagination must be devised. This may explain the part played by such externals as special garments, decorated vestments, and all sorts of pompous externals in the popular display of spiritual power. Considered apart from particular symbolic functions, these decorative externals might not be necessary if the authority that they express were armed with means of coercion. But the spiritual power *qua* spiritual has no means of coercion. Remove from it these decorative externals, and either new methods of acting upon imaginations must be devised, or it must be assumed that authority can exercise its functions with less assistance from the imagination. Consider also the constant decline of the conspicuous externals of authority in the temporal life of modern societies. This very striking process seems to admit of more than one interpretation. For one thing, the efficaciousness of coercive procedures has much increased; decorative externals are less needed when coercion, or the constant expectation of ever-ready coercive procedures, makes the presence of authority constantly felt.

There may well also be an intellectualization of the relation between authority and its subjects, which intellectualization would render the operation of the loud-speaking externals of authority impossible, whether these externals are replaced by something else or not. This seems to be a process of maturation fraught with great difficulties, for it seems to mean that when the image-creating power of these externals is not replaced, say, by more efficacious means of coercion, it has to be dispensed with anyway. So far as the Church is concerned, all this suggests that the externals should evolve from the crude expression of authority toward greater intellectuality in symbolic meaning.

That coercion does not pertain to the essence of authority but is only an instrument of it, is evidenced by the fact that coercion is only one of the instruments of authority. Persuasion is the other. Even in the case of the state, the decisions of authority are, most of the time, carried out by way of persuasion. This is where the analysis of the relations between coercion and persuasion proves useful. Many would be tempted to say that obedience to the state is always or almost always obtained through the threat of coercive procedures, though the actual use of coercion may be rare. State authority is ever ready to apply the overwhelming power of coercion where it is needed. What is in question is whether the importance of this power is exclusive. Much can be learned from the critical cases in which persuasion no longer works as an instrument of state authority, where, in other words, all the instrumental work has to be done by coercion. The general fact is that coercion itself does not work. In 1917 the Russian high command could no longer use the threat of supreme punishment to curb desertions because the men in charge of shooting deserters refused obedience. In this connection, the case of psychical coercion is quite particular and deserves a special investigation. No doubt, the methods of physical coercion do not work unless they are supported by a large amount of persuasion. The good thing about psychical coercion is that it makes persuasion, as well as physical coercion, unnecessary. The only limitation on a power employing intensive propaganda as an instrument of psychical coercion results from the imperfection of its methods. The automation of men and women is never absolute. The most bewildering miracles obtained by intensive propaganda presuppose a background of willingness to be coerced. This necessary background of willingness is made thinner by the intensity of propaganda, but it is not annihilated.

Let us now consider the features proper to political coercion. Clearly, the state is not the only society which uses some sort of coercive measures. When coercion is used as a distinguishing feature of civil government, some specifications are understood. For one thing, the forms of coercion that other societies are allowed are restricted. The state alone controls such extreme methods of coercion as life imprisonment and the death penalty. Clearly, the severity of coercive measures may be restricted by decisions of the government; thus, the death penalty has been abolished in some countries. It is not inconceivable that life imprisonment should also be held unnecessary in some times and places. But whether the heaviest penalties are more or less severe, the feature of decisive significance is that their severity is determined by no other power than that of the state. There are indeed societies which give the head of the family coercive powers including capital punishment: by common interpretation those societies are still in a primitive stage of development in which an incompletely constituted state does not yet assert its monopoly on unrestricted methods of coercion.

Secondly, the power of coercion claimed by the state is

such that its effects cannot be avoided by resignation of membership. Many associations use penalties to enforce discipline. So long as membership is voluntary, coercion is conditional. State coercion is not conditioned by voluntary membership. Whoever emigrates from one republic immigrates into another republic, and whoever runs away from the coercive power of one government falls under the coercive power of another government. Withdrawal into the wilderness is a purely accidental possibility which becomes increasingly rare as the maturation of mankind leaves few areas of the earth outside the boundaries of the state. These two characteristics of coercion, namely, its admitting of no restrictions, except those set by the state itself, and its inescapability, are summed up with sufficient clarity by the expression "unconditioned coercion."

It is proper for us now to ask whether the instrument of unconditioned coercion constitutes the defining characteristic of the state. Countless expositors hold, and more of them understand, that the state is properly defined by the power of unconditional coercion. This implies that where the instrument of coercion is unneeded, the state is equally unneeded. A community made up exclusively of virtuous and enlightened persons would need no coercive methods. Accordingly, it is commonly held that in such a community there would be no state, no civil government. The least that can be said of this implication is that it cannot be taken for granted. It is by no means obvious that the authority needed in a community of ideally good persons would not have the character of a republic.

It is also implied that in the constitution of the state, unconditioned coercion is not preceded by any more primary and basic features. It suffices to consider this second implication in relation to what was said on coercion as an *instrument*, to see that coercion cannot serve to define the essence of the state, although it may be used to characterize the state as a property following upon its essence. When we come to the question whether civil government necessarily involves the power of unconditioned coercion, the answer follows this line: in a society, say, mankind in the state of original innocence, where coercive procedures are unneeded, the essence of civil government is not accompanied by coercive instruments because the latter are unneeded, but it has within itself the foundation of unconditioned coercion and involves a readiness to develop coercive instruments whenever they happen to be needed. It would be quite exact to say that civil government, by reason of the kind of good which it pursues, possesses the instrument of unconditioned coercion either formally or virtually. So far as formal possession is concerned, civil government is theoretically separable from unconditioned coercion, but not so far as virtual possession is concerned. An instrument cannot constitute a defining feature for the obvious reason that its instrumental nature presupposes a constitution and the definability of a principal cause relative to a definite purpose.

Without providing a definition of the state, the consideration of coercion may lead to it in the way in which a property leads to an essence. An examination of the purposes of state coercion may be a very safe way to the very essence of the state. One of the most common and enduring features of liberalism is the theory that coercion cannot have any other purpose than the protection of society against evildoers. At the time of its greatest audacity liberalism could dream of a state of affairs in which the government would have no function besides the repression of actions harmful to others. If only it is assumed, further, that such a state of affairs decreases the number of opportunities for unsocial behavior, this liberal limitation of the state could be accompanied by a hope, as well as an ideal, of anarchy. It is important to remark that, in order to restrict the state to the coercion of evildoers, it is necessary to postulate first that the coercion of evildoers has only one function, namely, the protection of honest people. If it is granted that state coercion aims not only at the protection of honest people but also at the moral good of the evildoer—whether actual or potential—it becomes immediately impossible to hold that the state is only an agency for the coercion of rebellious persons.[7]

The problem of decisive significance is whether state coercion, which is obviously designed to procure peace for law-abiding persons, is also designed to bring about a good moral situation in the evildoer himself. To the theory that state coercion has a pedagogical function, it is commonly objected, with rather cheap irony, that virtue, being essentially related to voluntariness, cannot be procured from without. This platitude is perfectly true and totally irrelevant, for the relevant question is not whether the perfection of voluntary action can be procured from without, which is obviously impossible, but rather whether action from without can favor the development or the preservation of virtuous voluntariness by removing obstacles or preventing their formation.

Let us consider a series of situations beginning with coercion applied to an actual evildoer and ending with the relation of coercion to men of good will and good habits. Here is, to begin with, a man who, because of the actual commission of a crime, is forcibly placed in a position where such bad action cannot be committed for a long time. In the

---

[7] "St. Thomas in the commentaries on the *Nicomachean Ethics*," wrote Professor Simon, "seems to define the state by unconditioned coercion. He shows that coercion by the state has not only a protective but also a pedagogical function. Thus we are led to a notion of the state in terms of completeness. This is a most regular logical procedure, going from what is less essential but more directly noticeable to what is directly noticeable but more essential." Excerpt from manuscript on "Coercion in Civil Society."

attempt to reform him the ratio of failure may be high, but from this it does not follow that successful reformation, even though infrequent, should be considered an unimportant purpose. Next to the man who actually committed a crime, there is the would-be criminal, generally a young fellow, who certainly would fall into crime if he were not restrained by the fear of punishment. Such restraint procured by fear may spare him bad habits at the age when the most significant habits are formed and take him safely beyond the critical period into phases of life where the temptation of crime is easier to defeat. It can safely be said that the case so described is that of the majority, or of a large minority, of the men who mature in habits of good behavior. Next comes the case of men who have never felt the temptation of crime or felony, but are so disposed that they will soon experience it if the coercive power of society breaks down. War and revolutions supply many examples of the disasters which threaten men of perfectly normal habits when familiar fears no longer supplement their determination to be good. These fears are never spoken of. They are not given much conscious attention, yet they act efficaciously in the silence of their familiar presence. Under violently upset circumstances, it is discovered with amazement that the will power of ordinary men (which proved sufficient under ordinary circumstances, that is, under circumstances including the threat of coercive procedures) is weaker than it was believed to be. Things whose ownership appears in the least uncertain are quickly appropriated by men who never had stolen and who used to feel sure that they never would. Sooner or later the same men take part in the general looting and perhaps in worse felonies.

Farther on the side of ethical spontaneity, let us consider the men of really high morality, who can be safely expected to abide by their principles even if all fear of punishment disappeared. Men of such high moral standards are few in any society. In order to reach the high level of morality where they are supposed to be, these good men needed to be taught and trained. Let us ask the question of the use of coercion by political society with regard to what is best in society, that is, the small minority of distinguished persons who are so stabilized in good behavior that they really do not need to be coerced or threatened with coercion. The question is whether the state's power of coercion had anything to do with the training of these men in moral excellence. Just go over the conceivable factors of such moral excellence. The exhortations and examples of closely related individuals are indeed of great significance. But common experiences show how limited the power of personal influence is. In periods of rapid historical movements especially, it is common to see young people caught in sociological streams and wandering irresistibly away from personal influence. Besides the influence of particular persons, that of the spiritual power certainly plays a great role in the training of men in moral excellence. To have an idea of the limits of this influence, consider the testimony of the spiritual power itself. Its constant concern for the institutions and mores of the secular society is the most convincing evidence that training in moral excellence is not done by the spiritual power alone but is effected in a very important measure by temporal and secular society. Within the temporal and secular society, great influence is exercised in favor of good moral training by associations of entirely voluntary character—sporting, recreational, and others —which use hardly any kind of coercion. Great influence belongs also to less voluntary institutions, such as schools where only mild forms of coercion are used. All these influences are ultimately grounded in the stability procured by the power of unconditioned coercion.

To bring up distinguished personalities to act out of love for the good, without needing to be threatened, takes a great deal of liberty, indeed: liberty on the part of persons whose particular influence may convey to a young soul the call of lofty ideals; liberty on the part of voluntary associations. All this needed liberty rests on the firm basis of obligations sanctioned by unconditioned coercion. Can it be said that in society as well as within the individual person liberty must rest on a basis of necessity? Unconditioned coercion would be the basis of necessity on which all the liberties at work in the training of the loftiest souls are grounded. To ascertain the conditions in which this view holds, consider (1) the nature of the liberties at work: these are liberties already shaped by good moral qualities; (2) the character of the liberties that are acted upon: these are still able to make wrong choices. This should be the basis of the issue: political coercion is ultimately necessary by reason of the power to make wrong choices; liberty is necessary on account of the very nature of moral progress; coercion is necessary as an ultimate guarantee against the power of making wrong choices. The case seems ultimately to come down to this: the problem to be solved by unconditional coercion is the substitution of a sort of necessity for the freedom of choice which is the weak point of human freedom, namely, the freedom to choose between right and wrong.

Is coercion the only kind of necessity that society applies as a safeguard against the power of choosing the wrong? It is easy to see how society helps in other and loftier ways to eliminate the wrong choices, but it remains to be seen whether these other and loftier methods are all methods of liberty, akin to the virtues which, in the individual soul, increase freedom as they gradually rule out the possibility of wrong choices. When all that is cleared up, it should be possible to set principles relative to the proper amount of coercion. These principles should be expressive of antinomies. On the one hand, the way to wrong choice can never be altogether or wisely blocked; on the other hand, to exclude the possibility of a wrong choice often is also to exclude that of right choices and to rule out the good of more complete voluntariness. The wrong choice can be excluded either from without (coercion) or from within (virtue). There is a problem of timing, just as in the case of servile fear and filial fear. The lower method (coercion) is not annihilated, but remains virtually present in the higher.

It is relevant to inquire into the reasons why the liberal tradition is so steadily opposed to acknowledging this pedagogical function of political coercion. This can be described as follows:

(1) the liberal mind generally favors an idealistic interpretation of ethics which ignores or minimizes the role of material causality. Clearly, it is on the material part of moral life that coercion exercises its influence. Dispositions pertaining to the material side of human affairs may be less significant on higher than on lower levels of perfection; but even on the highest levels they do not become insignificant. A soldier possessed of a genuine virtue of fortitude still needs the material disposition called physical courage; if, as a result of emotional disturbances, his physical courage breaks down, his virtue of fortitude, no matter how genuine, may be confronted by insuperable difficulties. No doubt the fear of severe punishment contributes to the maintenance of physical courage even in the bravest men.

(2) In close connection with this idealistic tendency to disregard the significance of material causality, the liberal mind is generally inclined to apply to the earlier phases and lower levels of a perfection the laws which hold for the later phases and higher levels of the same perfection. It is true that perfect virtue acts out of love rather than out of fear; but from this it does not follow that incipient virtue is not normally helped by fear. It is equally mistaken to apply to the

later phases the law of the earlier and to ignore the law proper to the earlier phases—which is really the same as to disregard the existence of earlier phases.

St. Thomas approaches the necessity of man-made law from the angle of the functions of coercion.[8] If coercion is needed for the reasons we have given, it must be the instrument of a man-made law. This is the crucial point. Consider the cases in which coercion is not the instrument of a law. Then its name is violence. Violence is often unethical, but not necessarily. There are cases of just violence, for instance, in self-defense. Notice, further, that violence shares in the unconditioned character of state coercion; in self-defense, just violence may involve death. Thus the problem is to show how violence *normally* fails to achieve the purposes of coercion, and how coercion in the hands of any society which is not a political society fails to achieve its purposes. Thus we are led to the definition of political society in terms of completeness.

Civil Society Defined

The preceding discussion has shown that unconditioned coercion, being only an instrument of civil society, cannot supply the means of defining the state. The definition of a community must proceed from the purpose and/or the good aimed at by the men who associate in this community. The common good of a community is its object as well as its end.

Let us follow the method of Aristotle. He starts with the consideration of human needs in daily life. The community where these needs are satisfied is the family or the household. The primary attention given to needs does not signify that the satisfaction of individual needs is the only purpose of communities. The household as understood by Aristotle is

[8] St. Thomas Aquinas, *Sum. Theol.*, 1a 2ae, q. 92, 1 and 2, says man-made law is necessary as a means of coercion.

supposed to be self-sufficient with regard to all the needs of daily life. It is much more inclusive than the family as we understand it; or, more exactly, the family as understood by Aristotle is in charge of many functions that have been taken away from it in modern societies. Roughly, the needs described as pertaining to daily life in Aristotle's theory of the household are: shelter, food—but this involves the growth of crops as well as cooking and serving—the upbringing of children, and the care of the sick. An entirely normal household in the sense of Aristotle is an organization self-sufficient in all these respects. It comprises, besides an agricultural enterprise, a variety of workshops. Concerning the notion of self-sufficiency, let it be remarked that there is no question of any group being self-sufficient in all respects and unqualifiedly. In the case of the household as well as that of civil society, self-sufficiency must be understood in terms of an ideal and of a tendency. It can be said, for instance, that the tendency of our societies is to depend more and more on food-processing plants for the preparation of food, on garment factories for clothing, on hospitals for the care of the sick, and on theatres for recreation. The self-sufficiency of the household in Aristotle's theory designates the opposite tendency. Insofar as the household achieves self-sufficiency, persons can stay home and have all they need in daily life. Again, the emphasis on needs, which is indispensable in the introductory phases of the treatment of a community, does not signify that the household, or any community properly so-called, exists only for the sake of satisfying individual needs. A household is a cooperative system in which the general laws of the common good and its primacy are verified.

Thus we can represent the household by a circle and say that, so far as the needs of daily life are concerned, no one has to trespass the limits of this circle. But beyond the needs and the goods of daily life, there is a universe of human goods which can be briefly described as pertaining to the noble life, that is, to a life of culture and contemplation. For the satisfaction of these needs and the attainment of these goods, persons have to trespass the limits of the household. The question "How far do they have to go?" leads directly to the definition of political society. Having crossed the boundaries of the household, we may find ourselves in a group of households where new cooperatives are organized and still be far from meeting the requirements of a noble life. The township of Aristotle is capable of satisfying human needs better than the household itself, yet it falls short of the totality of human good that a noble life requires.

With the transition of the household to the township we are confronted for the first time by the problem of the opposition between the private and the public.[9] My suggestion would be that this opposition can be explained only in terms of polarity. The pole of the public is constituted by civil society, the pole of the private by the household, more precisely by the family, and still more precisely by the couple. A group of households placed in the vicinity of each other for no purpose pertaining directly to family life—this is the point that is hard to specify—insofar as it constitutes an association, is relative to features that find their climax in political society. If, on the contrary, neighboring households are grouped by reason of kinship, the group retains a private character and cannot be described as a township. It may be very significant

[9] The manuscript of Professor Simon on "Civil Society Defined" attributes to George Gurvitch the view that it is impossible to define private law and public law. This line of argumentation is particularly conspicuous in Gurvitch's early work, L'Idée du Droit Social, p. 13, where it is said: "The traditional opposition between public law and private law is not founded on any factual criterion and varies with the changing will of the state which at different times gives the advantage to one zone of the law or another. . . ." This position is a first step in Gurvitch's subsequent treatment of social reality as a dynamic system.

to remark that economic enterprises, no matter how large, can retain a private character. Even if the number of the associates in an economic enterprise is very large, it retains a private character which sharply contrasts with the public character of the smallest township. Ownership is not, all by itself, a decisive factor. The goods of an association may be owned collectively by any number of members without this association ceasing to be private. The goods of a village are also owned collectively by the villagers, but the meaning of their *collective* ownership is quite different. What is it that makes the difference if not the contrast between the direction toward the perfection of daily life and the perfection of the noble life? The smallest village, insofar as it is distinct from a patriarchal group of related families, is an institution on the way toward the perfection of the noble life. An economic enterprise, no matter how large, may be related to the goods of daily life. If an economic enterprise serves directly and properly the civil community, it may still remain private. But its being private seems to be accidental. The key to the whole question of the public versus the private may be found in the comparison of economic enterprises working for the household and economic enterprises working for civil society. All this is merely tentative.

Let the township be symbolized by a circle concentric to that of the household. In order to obtain all that is needed for the noble life, it is necessary to trespass the still narrow circle of the household. A circle whose limit need not be trespassed in the pursuit of the goods of the noble life symbolizes political society.

Here again it is necessary to bear in mind a judicious understanding of self-sufficiency. Aristotle refers to the Greek city-state, a unit small in size and in membership. He certainly recommends that all the goods of the noble life be made available within the boundaries of the city. But clearly no city has ever achieved self-sufficiency in an unqualified fashion, and what holds for the small Greek city-state holds also for kingdoms and empires. In our times world exchanges and relations of interdependence on a world scale are such that it has been held that the only possible state in the sense of Aristotle would be a world state. This is perfectly certain, but the possibility of a world state does not follow therefrom.[10] Rather, what follows is the conclusion that no political society is entirely faithful to its type inasmuch as its type involves self-sufficiency. Experience shows that the constitution of political society admits of degrees of sufficiency. Thus, when classical views on the self-sufficiency of the state are applied to American society, they split, as it were, between functions pertaining to the several states and functions pertaining to the federal government. The League of Nations and the United Nations, in spite of all the rhetoric about the preservation of sovereign rights, express unmistakably the realization that most important human needs find satisfaction neither in a unitary state nor in a federal union, but demand the constitution of a community broader than either of them. If such

[10] In a separate memorandum included among his manuscripts Professor Simon commented on the idea of world government. A portion of the memorandum is as follows:

"As we read history, we can distinguish periods and areas in which political units were much less incomplete than in other periods and areas. Today the proponents of a world government have no trouble showing that any community whose boundaries do not coincide with those of the world falls short, by a disastrously great distance, of the completeness that the notion of the state implies. From this it does not necessarily follow that a world state is possible, whether now or in any explorable part of the future, but it may follow that the incompleteness of our political communities has to be imperfectly remedied, over an indefinitely long period, by a variety of small-scale measures, with little hope of removing the threats that result from the gap between our political needs and the actual possibilities of political organization."

See also Robert M. Hutchins, *St. Thomas and the World State* (Milwaukee: Marquette University Press, 1949).

an organization as that of the United Nations proves successful, a day will come when it should be said that the notion of political society, so far as the United States is concerned, divides into three systems of functions: those of the several states, those of the federal union, and those of the United Nations.

Within the circle of civil society, the things that remain private and the things that are of the state as directly managed by it should be treated in terms of a double problem of autonomy. Experience shows that some functions may, without their object being missed, be assumed either by public services or by private enterprise. Inasmuch as there is a general subordination of the private to the public, the principle of autonomy requires that what can be done well by private means be left to private responsibility. Then, within the system of public institutions, there is a subordination of such units as townships and cities to such larger units as counties, provinces, and states. The issue of centralization versus decentralization generally concerns the problem of autonomy within the system of the public institutions. Here, the principle of autonomy requires that what can be done well by the smaller and lower unit be never taken over by the larger one. The systematic observance of the principle of autonomy leaves comparatively few functions to direct management by the political authorities. This is the deep meaning of Jefferson's statement: "The best government is that which governs least." [11]

[11] As is evident from the writings of Yves Simon, he is passionately and intellectually attached to the idea of autonomy in its political significance. For him political autonomy means strong local government and strong social communities. His kinship with Thomas Jefferson and de Tocqueville is clear. In his notes he recorded many passages from Jefferson supporting the idea of local authority. The following one is taken from a letter of Thomas Jefferson written July 15, 1790:

"Every man and every body of men on earth, possesses the right

Let us, for the sake of clarity, assume that the sufficiency which defines the state is actually realized in one organization. Thus we suppose that there is no division of the type embodied in the relation of an individual state to a federal union. A third circle concentric to those of the household and of the township symbolizes the society within which not only the needs of daily life, but also those of the noble life, are entirely satisfied. Let us now try to see in what sense the satisfaction of those needs can be attributed to the state.

---

of self-government. They receive it with their being from the hand of nature. Individuals exercise it by their single will; collections of men by that of their majority; for the law of the majority is the natural law of every society of men." The same author years later wrote:
"[But] it is not by the [consolidation, or] concentration of powers, but by their distribution, that good government is effected. Were not this great country already divided into States, that division must be made, that each might do for itself directly, and what it can so much better do than a distant authority. Every state again is divided into counties, each to take care of what lies within its local bounds; each county again into townships or wards, to manage minute details: and every ward into farms, to be governed by its individual proprietor. Were we directed from Washington when to sow, and when to reap, we should soon want bread. It is by this partition of cares, descending in gradation from general to particular, that the mass of human affairs may be best managed, for the good and prosperity of all."
See *The Papers of Thomas Jefferson*, Vol. 17 (Princeton, N.J.: Princeton University Press, 1964), p. 195. Also see Saul K. Padover, *The Complete Jefferson* (New York: Duell, Sloan and Pearce, 1943), pp. 173–74.
Simon also included in his notes a quotation from Lord Acton, *Essays on Freedom and Power* (Glencoe, Ill.: Free Press, 1948), pp. 147–48:
". . . true republicanism is the principle of self-government in the whole and in all the parts. In an extensive country it can prevail only by the union of several independent communities in a single confederacy, as in Greece, in Switzerland, in the Netherlands, and in America; so that a large republic is not founded on a single city, like Rome and Paris, and, in a less degree, Athens, Berne, and Amsterdam; or, in other words, a great democracy must either sacrifice self-government to unit, or preserve it by federalism."

Considering the needs that can be satisfied by private initiative, the self-sufficiency of the state means, first of all, that its topographical boundaries comprise the whole series of the functions distinguished by the general process of the division of labor. For instance, the lack of industrial development, under modern circumstances, would be an insuperable obstacle to the constitution of a state. A country whose resources, equipment, and training are exclusively or almost exclusively agricultural, may possess the legal structure of a state, in fact it falls short of the sufficiency that the notion of the state implies; it would be, in more or less disguised ways, the protectorate of a better equipped neighbor.

With regard to the nature of the functions of private initiative, the relevant problem is whether they all are economic in character. In order to specify properly the notion of economic activity, it suffices, in the present context, to posit a relation to wealth and to recall that in a usage free from metaphor not all things which contribute to the good of man are wealth, but only those which, being external to man, have the character of mere means without any desirability of their own. With these specifications in mind, let us say that the functions in private hands are not all economic. Over and above all that pertains to the production and distribution of wealth, there are functions relative to the health of man and functions relative to his intellectual development. Medicine may be taken over by public services and exercised as a public function. This is as accidental as it would be in the case of nationalized agriculture, and what holds for medicine holds for scientific and historical research, teaching and all communication of knowledge. A more difficult problem concerns functions whose object is neither the health nor the intellectual development of man, but the training of human character. Character training is effected in part within the household. When it is not contained within the household, does it retain the character of a private function? It is strongly suggested that when character training is not a task of the family, it becomes a task of the church.

From the point of view of society at large, there is an essential difference between a farm which grows food for consumption of the farming family and a farm which supplies food to the public. In the case of the production of food for family consumption, all is private: initiative, management, and enjoyment, *potestas procurandi et dispensandi* as well as *usus*. As soon as products are delivered to the market, agriculture serves the public and becomes public so far as its finality is concerned. It might be wise to describe two series of functions pertaining to private initiative, those that are contained within private groups with regard to all the parts of their cycle, and functions that are public with regard to their ultimate phases. So far as economic functions are concerned, the factor of division is the market. But this division does not hold only for economic functions. Taking care of the sick is not an economic function; however, in relation to the contrast between the private and the public, there is a world of difference between taking care of the sick at home and in a public hospital.

Besides clearing up the relation "civil society" to economic functions—there is no reason why this so-called civil society should comprise only persons engaged in economic activities, but economists often use an arbitrarily broad concept of economics. Consider this problem: do the members of the "civil society" make up a society independently of the state organization? In other words, does the organization of civil society consist in state organization? The answer seems to be that the coincidence is not complete. There certainly are, in civil society, aspects of organization which do not coincide with state organization. Concerning those aspects of organization distinct from the state, the first problem is whether they are purely contractual or have a character of community. The tendency of the economist is certainly to interpret the organization of civil society in terms of contractual relations. This is one of the distinctive features of the utopia of economic liberalism. The reality is different, but what matters is the question of tendencies. What is signified by the tendency to reduce the organization of civil society to a system of contractual relations? This is a tentative answer: an organization of the community type is already needed on the level of civil society. If it is not established there, it will be lacking, or it will have to be supplied by the state. On the other hand, it seems that community organizations cannot on the level of civil society transcend their own plurality. Civil society may conceivably have a great number of foci or organizations. But it is only within the community form supplied by the state that civil society assumes unity. If, along the line of Berth, we speak of a strongly organized civil society as a guarantee against the imperialism of the state, let its organization always be conceived as pluralistic.

To sum up: "To be contained within the state" so far as these private functions are concerned, expresses more than mere presence within the topographic and jurisdictional limits of the state. To show *from what* we are distinguishing this "way of being contained," we can compare it with the meaning of such a proposition as "within the boundaries of such and such a country you find a great variety of soils, of climates, of spontaneous vegetations and of mineral deposits." Soils, climates, vegetation and mineral deposits are not modified by the contingency of being enclosed within a certain border. On the contrary, the private functions that we have been describing are modified by the form of community supplied by the state.

Consider now the functions that are public in character. A sharp distinction must be made between the functions public by essence and those that are public only by accident. It is by accident that the production and distribution of electricity are managed by a city administration. The functions public by essence have a character of totality, and they are relative to use. But this subject is better treated in relation to the function that is public *par excellence*, that of the state. What we have to show here is in what sense public functions exercised by such units as the township, the country, etc., are contained in the state. Their way of being contained in the state is describably in terms of a higher degree of information by the unity of community supplied by the state. Working from the bottom up, it should perhaps be observed first that the organization of these functions is always of a community type.

The Good of Civil Society

Let us now come to the question whether the good aimed at by civil society is a moral good. Concerning the relation of politics to morality, we can define three fundamental positions: (1) The good of civil society is not of a moral or ethical character, and in case of conflict between what is politically good and what is ethically good, the political must prevail and the ethical must yield. (2) The good pursued by civil society is of an ethical character. But what is ethically good must rule. In case of conflict the political must yield to the ethical. (3) The good aimed at by civil society is predominantly, i.e., more formally, a moral good. Accordingly, a conflict between ethical and political requirements cannot be final. It can be apparent, and the appearances can be strong, and going beyond the appearances may be extremely difficult. Yet, by reason of the intrinsically moral character of the political good, the notion of a service done to the civil community, save in purely accidental fashion by moral and lawful means, is contradictory. We say "save in purely accidental fashion," for, in the order of accidental causality the wrong may be the cause of the right and anything may cause anything.

To determine whether a good is intrinsically moral or not, let us consider the relation between perfection in nature and perfection in human use. The problem of the ethical situation of civil and political affairs can be phrased as follows: are the goods aimed at by the state organization goods of nature or goods of use? With regard to method this at least is clear: some aspects of completeness, entirety, and totality may not be so described without an already established reference to use. Yet the problem of use should not be tackled before every aspect of completeness, etc., describable without reference to use, has been actually described.

It is indispensable to go over the principles concerning nature and use.[12] Let us proceed by an analysis of examples

[12] Yves Simon frequently returned to a discussion of a philosophy of use as part of his analyses of the relations of thought and action. The passage here is a summary of this philosophy which he elaborated in *Philosophy of Democratic Government, ibid,* pp. 268–88.

In a set of unedited notes highly relevant to a theory of political community on "Social Communion and the Uncommunicability of Prudence" (a text made available to me by Mrs. Paule Simon), Professor Simon suggested that it would be worthwhile to develop Bergson's theory of society as present within the individual. He went on to say: "Beyond whatever is metaphorical in such an explanation, there is a real presence [of society within the individual —Ed.] inasmuch as there is unanimity of judgment in relation to a common object of action and an awareness of this unity. Society is present not only inasmuch as it is known and not only inasmuch as its good is willed but also inasmuch as the inclinations of all are, and are known and felt to be one with the demands of the common good. . . . In the case of affective communion the presence of society is realized by an operation which is elicited by the individual himself. . . . In the case of government by one leader, the non-accidental character of the unity of the cause is guaranteed by the individual unity of the leader. In the case of majority government, the nonaccidental character of the unity of the cause is guaranteed starting with things external to man. A car may be in good shape or in poor shape. It is possible to make a good use of a good car and a bad use of a good car and a bad use of a poor car and a good use of a poor car. Notice that from the point of view of the relation to use, works of art obey the same law as things of nature. What was said of a car would hold in the same sense and degree of a horse or anything of nature subjected to human use. Such things comprise the human body and its parts as well as the powers of the human soul. It is possible to make a good use of an organism in good health, and a good use of a diseased organism, etc. Likewise, a good eyesight and a poor eyesight, a good memory and a bad memory, a keen intellect and a dull intellect are things of which it is possible to make good use and bad use. In the will itself there is a goodness of nature distinct from goodness of use. What we call a good will is a will dedicated to good use. But, apart from use, a will is strong or weak, and it is possible to make a good and a bad use both of a strong will and of a weak will.

Examples designed to indicate the distinction between goodness of nature and goodness of use seem to evidence also a law of mutual independence and mutual indifference between goodness of nature and goodness of use. Indeed, in no

---

by the constitutional arrangement which excludes a tie vote. In unanimity by way of affective communion, the nonaccidental character of the unity of the cause is guaranteed: (a) by the unity of the common good and of the way leading to it, (b) by universal dedication to the common good and by the unity of reliable information. . . . What is devoid of guaranty is this basic hypothesis: that the community will always be made up exclusively of well intentioned and well informed persons. . . . Unity by affective communion may be (a) extremely rare, (b) always incomplete . . . and (c) extremely precarious. They nevertheless enjoy unique significance in the life of society because in them social life attains a unique degree of intensity and awareness. This can be likened to the significance in individual life of short and precarious and rare moments of intense happiness forcefully set off by a background of misfortune, e.g., liberation from oppression, reunion after a long separation, etc."

case does natural excellence entail good use or natural deficiency result necessarily in bad use. However, there are cases in which a natural deficiency constitutes an obstacle to good use. This is noticeable in the case of some things external to man; thus, a car whose brakes are not in working order admits of no good use except in extraordinary circumstances. I say that in such a case natural deficiency is an obstacle to good use. There is a case in which a natural deficiency is more than an obstacle to good use and has the character of a tendency toward bad use. It is the case of the sense appetite. True, a man may be afflicted with diseased emotions without doing anything wrong in the order of use. But, more definitely than a car whose brakes are poor, some perverse emotions are things that admit of no good use. The proper use of human freedom in its dealing with unnatural and perverse emotions is to uproot them if possible, and if not, to curb them; in short, to deny them existence insofar as it is in the power of human freedom. But, by reason of the basic relation of the appetite to existence, emotions are things that strive toward actualization; consequently, emotions whose voluntary actualization necessarily involves an act of bad use constitute a positive tendency toward bad use. This tendency is not necessitating. When emotions, whether normal or perverse, attain the intensity of compulsions, their actualization and the actualization of their consequences are necessary, but there no longer is use, for use implies a mastery that compulsion denies.

Thus, the relation between goodness of nature and goodness of use can be summed up as follows: (1) they are really distinct in all cases, (2) in some cases goodness of nature is indifferent to goodness of use inasmuch as it does not make it more or less probable, (3) there are cases in which a deficiency of nature constitutes an obstacle to good use, (4) in the sense appetite and only there, a natural deficiency may constitute a positive tendency toward bad use.

This enumeration leaves out an important point: that the tendency toward perfection in the order of use generally involves a tendency to seek perfection in the order of nature. One can make a good use of a poor intellect, but whoever is determined to make a good use of his intellect seeks to improve it, though not necessarily in all directions. It would be relevant to show what principles restrict the tendency to seek natural perfection.

The question of the ethical situation of the state is identical with the question whether the good of civil society is a good of nature or a good of use. This question is identical with the question whether political society is a work of prudence or a work of art, that is, belongs to the order of good action or to the order of successful creation. The need for arts subservient to political prudence is not in question. Political wisdom is in fact served by a multiplicity of arts. The problem is whether dispositions of the nature of art play only an instrumental part, no matter how important, or play the part of principal cause of the civil and political good and constitute political wisdom.[13]

[13] In other comments on practical wisdom Professor Simon spoke about the problem of the relationship between thought and action. He wrote as follows: "As far as action is concerned what matters primarily is fulfillment, not explanation, and it is within an adherence firm enough to insure fullfillment that the search for explanation must be pursued. . . . The man of practical wisdom well knows that what matters is to do what is right rather than to understand why it is right. He also knows that what ought to be done is not really done unless it is brought into existence according to the mode proper to a rational agent. . . . Practical wisdom itself requires that the science of ethics enlightens the minds of men."

6

Pessimism
and the Philosophy
of Progress

As THE DEFEAT OF THE TOTALITARIAN STATES in World War II made it more than ever necessary that democratic enthusiasm be revived, and at the same time created conditions favorable to its rebirth, the problems represented by the opposition of optimism and pessimism acquire an especial immediacy.* Optimism, pessimism—a philosopher feels embarrassed to write the words, which are so often used at random and which tend to arouse confusion. But let us beware: effective ideas, the ideas which have the greatest and most en-

* Substantially identical with the chapter of the same title in *Community of the Free* (New York: Holt, 1947).

during influence upon human events, are often confused ideas. Thanks to their very confusion, they find an easy entrance into the half-rational sphere which is the nursery of general attitudes, states of mind, ideas relative to the future and to the meaning of history, emotional judgments upon doctrines, parties, movements, and leaders. Commonly, it is confused ideas which make up the doctrinal substance of the great creative and destructive enthusiasms, of myths and mysticisms. The philosopher who would understand what takes place in the obscure centers of the mind where systematic thought, by mingling with images and emotions, exercises its influence upon the actual future of societies, will attach extreme importance to understanding certain confused ideas. Instead of laughing at them on the ground that they are confused, he will exert his powers to clarify them.

Let us turn back to the palmy days of classic democracy. It was then universally admitted that democracy demands an optimistic concept of human nature and history. Friends and enemies of democracy agreed in saying that government of the people by the people presupposes a "great act of confidence" in the wisdom of the common man, in the capacity of the greater part of mankind to prefer the general interest to private interests. It was also admitted—or, rather, it was taken for granted—that faith in democracy demands an act of confidence in the benevolent activity of a genius of history able secretly to organize the scattered initiatives of individuals in such a way that they should make for the greatest good of the greatest number.

Circumstances at the period were favorable to optimism. The conquest of the physical world by science and techniques was progressing at ever-increasing speed. Instruments of learning, in many ways superior to any that had been available to the great minds of the past, were available to everyone. Great political and social phenomena—perhaps actually less new than was thought—persistently prompted the conviction that humanity, at last reaching maturity of thought and will at the very moment when it was consolidating its dominion over the physical world, was now master of its own history. The new, unified great powers represented striking forms of order well calculated to fire men's imaginations and to spread the idea that decisive progress had been made in creating order in human life. Persuasive experiments had revealed that the field open to rational initiative in the realm of historical construction was incomparably larger than had been thought in the recent past. When Joseph de Maistre learned that the Americans had decided to build a federal capital which should bear the name of Washington, he did not hesitate to predict the failure of an enterprise so obviously in contradiction to all the certainties of his traditionalist, reactionary, and pessimistic philosophy. The building of a city is not a thing which it is given to man to decide upon. Yet the experiment succeeded, and it was successfully imitated. Through all the period of classic democracy, the whole world kept an amazed and attentive eye upon what was happening in the United States, the first great nation which owed its birth not to the hazards of a play of forces but to the conscious decision of human beings. Reflecting upon this prodigious widening of the possibilities offered to human initiative, men's minds became intoxicated with the feeling that humanity was escaping from the fatalities which had from the beginning of time governed its history.

At the same time new guarantees, clearer and doubtless more efficacious than the old ones, were being given for the protection of personal rights against the arbitrariness of power. Penal laws lost much of their traditional cruelty. As a result of technical progress and of legal reforms in the direction of social equality, well-being increased, at least in certain sections of society—in those classes, precisely, which contributed most to forming the collective conscience and spirit of the age. Finally—a particularly striking and particularly encouraging symptom—the western world enjoyed a long period of peace, the great peace of the nineteenth century, troubled only by circumscribed wars, the harmfulness of which seemed negligible compared with the great butcheries of earlier ages. So everything was going better; and one could believe that, to have everything go supremely well someday, all that was needed was to let things take their course. Taking into account the element of convention inevitably associated with attempts to delimit historical periods, it is possible to say that the era of classic democracy commences immediately after the fall of Napoleon and ends not long after the beginning of the First World War. Through all this period, democratic ideas, whether they were realized or not (and they were generally quite incompletely realized in political and social institutions), had the benefit of being in the order of the day, of being identified with the spirit of the age, of representing to the public mind the great conquering force to which the future was promised.

It would be easy, through that century of optimism, to find numerous manifestations of pessimism. What it is important to note is that the sincerest, the truest, the deepest expressions of pessimism during the era of classic democracy are referable to another age. Joseph de Maistre had numerous disciples, but his pessimism is the pessimism of a prophet of the past. Baudelaire's pessimism seems to us today to be an anticipation of ideas and feelings whose influence was not to be felt until much later. Expressions of pessimism which become fashionable and need only let themselves be borne by the general trend in order to gain wide currency, have these striking characteristics—they are superficial, secondhand, sophistic, and more or less insincere. We find them in Byron, Lamartine, Alfred de Vigny, Alfred de Musset, and their disciples. The great denouncer of democratic optimism, Georges Sorel, reproached these writers with having discredited pessimism:

At the beginning of the nineteenth century, there was such a concert of groaning that pessimism became odious. Poets, who were not, as a matter of fact, much to be pitied, professed to be victims of fate, of human wickedness, and still more of the stupidity of a world which had not been able to distract them. . . . When this fashion for imprecations had passed, sensible men began to ask themselves if all this display of pretended pessimism had not been the result of a certain want of mental balance.[1]

The situation was so unfavorable to pessimism that any profession of it which accorded with the public's idea of it inevitably ended in mere literary declamation.

The optimism of classic democracy found its clearest expression in a certain philosophy of progress. The decline of this philosophy coincided with the great crisis of democracy. The men of our generation have something to say about the history of the idea of progress during the time when democracy was no longer the order of the day. Immediately after the end of the First World War, our youthful minds were assailed by a host of influences hostile to any philosophy of progress. These influences were expressed in a confused or even in a contradictory way, but confusion and contradiction could only favor a criticism which was chiefly composed of irony, sarcastic rhetoric, derision, pride, and skillful appeals to the instinct of destruction. All the dogs of Voltaire's wit were once more loosed. One must laugh at progress, or else put up with the most unpleasant of affronts, that of passing for a fool. We all chose the easier branch of the alternative, with differing degrees of constancy and sincerity. By laughing at progress we spared ourselves many difficulties, we called attention to our intellectual distinction, we enjoyed ourselves.

[1] *Reflections on Violence,* translated by T. E. Hulme (New York: Peter Smith, 1941), p. 8. (First published in French in 1908.)

Then one fine day there sprang up fully armed before us men who believed only in nothing. The Revolution of Nihilism completed the liquidation of the nineteenth century. And what took place upon the ruins of the old beliefs and illusions was not, as so many fools had hoped, the building of a new order, but carnage incalculably vast. In the way of destructiveness, we had found our masters. But we had our share of responsibility in the work of destruction. Woe unto them who in shallowness of heart shall again commit a fault whose gravity has been proved by such events!

The Romantic Philosophy of Progress

The philosophy of progress which was in a sense the official doctrine of classic democracy (we shall hereafter call it the romantic philosophy of progress, or more briefly, the romantic philosophy) is far from being a strictly consistent system. It must be regarded as a historical *complexus* resulting from the more or less contingent association of several elements. Between these elements, analysis can find logical incompatibilities. But it often occurs that principles in logical opposition, by creating a state of tension through their very opposition, contribute to the vitality of a complex of ideas.

1. The influence of Rousseau is everywhere present. The many meanings of that influence become clear and classifiable when one notes that Rousseauan optimism is a completely and logically naturalistic doctrine, all of whose fundamental features are developments of some aspect of the idea of nature. Rousseau's naturalism has no place for the imagery of blind and implacable forces which haunts those moral and social systems which are tied to a mechanistic concept of the world. Rousseau, with a precise metaphysical sense, pictures every nature as a good thing which a benevolent Providence is

guiding towards a state of perfection. But truthfully to interpret the physical universe and the moral universe, it is indispensable to complete and balance the idea of nature by a set of opposite ideas, the ideas of contingency, of chance, of risk, of adventure, of precariousness, of disorder, of evil. Now, in Rousseau's mind the idea of nature invades the entire vision of the world, refuses to be held back, and although unable completely to absorb the opposite ideas, reduces them to a minimum. Disorder and evil, things foreign to a completely natural course of events, become paradoxical and scandalous things, explicable only by a catastrophe. That catastrophe is the fall of humanity into the servitude of society and the corruption of civilization.

The theory of an original catastrophe is in perfectly harmonious agreement with another characteristic of Rousseau's idea of nature. This all-invading idea is refractory to any inner differentiation, and in its passionate unity it confounds the picture of a state which is truly natural with that of a state which is simply native. Thus primitive life acquires all the privileges of the perfect life, an initial condition is treated as a terminal condition, and the existence of the blessed is confounded with the existence of savages. Finally, this exaltation of primitive life goes hand in hand with an exaltation of irrational nature. In a certain sense, nature is opposed to reason, and it is from nature understood in this sense that Rousseau's idea of natural goodness stems. Rousseau's naturalism comprises a theory of the primacy of those emotions and instincts which man shares with the animals.

In the romantic philosophy of progress, certain aspects of naturalism are generally masked under certain exactly opposite positions and tendencies. The romantic philosophy places the state of perfection in the future, not in the past. It proclaims the benefits of civilization, describes the barbarous past in the darkest terms. It is rationalistic, and, not content with affirming the pre-eminence of reason, it despises the irrational part of the human soul and singularly misunderstands its role in moral and social life. Nevertheless, it remains Rousseauan in a radical sense, inasmuch as it is pervaded by a notion of natural goodness, in which, despite appearances, all the features of Rousseau's naturalism are present in their purest form. Furthermore, the rationalistic component gives way from time to time under pressure from the naturalistic component, so that a thinker who at one moment was lauding reason and civilization, at another is attributing spotless virtue and infallible wisdom to the most primitive society, for no other reason than its primitive character.

In addition, it often happens that a rationalistic search for the most elaborate social structures—structures the farthest removed from primitive barbarism—is not too illogically combined with the exaltation of the most instinctive and most primitive sides of everlasting man. Under these circumstances Rousseau's philosophy undergoes a recasting which gives it a peculiar effectiveness. An eccentric thinker who had neither common sense nor genius nor scientific attainment immortalized himself by boldly incorporating Rousseau's naturalism into a social philosophy oriented entirely towards the future, with no retrospective imagery of any kind. Like Rousseau, Fourier reveres nature; like Rousseau, he despises civilization; but unlike Rousseau, he places the full flowering of nature not before civilization but beyond it. The age of civilization is only an intermediate phase—the last of the intermediate phases—between primitive savagery and the final "harmony." The entire task of reason, of the physical sciences and the social sciences, is to bring about the advent of harmony. Now, in Fourier's harmonious society it is easy to recognize a typical solution of the eternal problems which result from a peculiarity presented by the authority of instincts in the human species.

More numerous, richer, and more delicate than the instincts of animals, man's instincts are subject to a law of *insufficiency* which is well known to moralists. Man's instincts let loose desires connected with the conservation and expansion of individual life and social life, but they do not suffice to direct those desires. If instinct is left to itself, the desires to which it has given birth will fail of their object, produce discord, and arrest life. Reason, then, is forced to intervene; and through the moral virtues, through prudence, through authority, to subject to man's service the desires which instinct arouses but is incapable of controlling. The solution is burdensome; it implies mortification of desires, asceticism. Furthermore, it is precarious; for if once reason relaxes its hold, the emancipated desires will riot in murderous enterprises. Fourier's solution claims to be less burdensome and less precarious. Fourier admits without reservation that all the passions, considered in their very irrationality, in their instinctive primitiveness, are good, holy, loved of God. To submit them to any kind of pressure, to any kind of repression, is to do violence to nature and to offend its Author. And yet they must be prevented from destroying the individual and society, as experience shows that they tend to do. The danger is real in the civilized state; it disappears in the harmonious state, thanks to an arrangement of society so judicious that all the passions, including those which appear to us to be monstrous, can be given free rein without damage to anyone and to the great profit of each and all. The synthesis is complete. Fourier's philosophy is naturalistic, even more radically naturalistic than Rousseau's. It is irrationalistic and primitivistic, since, in the last analysis, it proposes the liberation of everything in man which lies beneath the level of the reason; it is rationalistic in a very profound sense, for the social arrangement designed to permit the enfranchisement of the passions by making them wholly beneficial is the work of rational, ponderated, lucid, scientific calculation. Lastly, Fourier's philosophy most definitely has the characteristics of a philosophy of progress.

If one studies the Fourieristic doctrine with all the incredibly fantastic plans for social organization in which its author's folly reveled, one is tempted to see in it an isolated phenomenon in the history of ideas, hardly representative, and of small importance. Thoroughgoing disciples of Fourier have never been numerous. But if one studies the essence of the Fourieristic doctrine, its fundamental answer to the problems posed by the antinomies of our nature, one percieves that, behind his delirious images, Fourier has given unusually precise expression to an idea which haunts any philosophy of progress that may be linked to an optimistic naturalism—the extremely seductive idea of substituting for the control of the passions by virtue, prudence, and authority, a judicious arrangement of social relations which makes the rigors of asceticism and obedience superfluous.

The complexity of the foregoing analysis has sufficiently shown that the naturalism of the romantic philosophy cannot easily be summed up in brief and precise formulas. In many cases, it has the character of a more or less secret inspiration, rather than that of an explicit doctrine. We now propose to describe the doctrinal elements whose formal and fully conscious expression appears currently amongst nineteenth-century theorists of progress.

2. First place belongs to the idea of the *necessity* of progress. But this idea admits of several forms and of several degrees. It may refer to a mere exigency, or to an exigency accompanied by a *de jure* necessity, or finally to an exigency accompanied by a *de jure* necessity and a *de facto* necessity.

By saying that progress is a necessary thing, one can merely mean that it is the object of an aspiration, of a demand, of an imperious exigency of human nature. If one means no more than this, it must be said that progress is necessary just as virtue is necessary—that is, as a *sine qua non* of man's fidelity to his vocation. What will actually happen? We do not know. All that we do know presents itself under the form of the relations between condition and thing conditioned. If humanity progresses, it obeys the law of its nature; if it does not progress, its natural law is transgressed. The idea of a progress which should be necessary only as a mere exigency does not permit us to go beyond these conditional propositions.

By saying that progress is a necessary thing, one can mean that it has not only, like virtue, the necessity of an exigency, but also the necessity of an essentially indefectible determination, like every process of proper causation in the physical world. Any causal law expresses the dynamism of a nature, and this dynamism is necessarily what it is, because of the very identity of the nature with itself. Thus, whatever be our definitions of the term *gas*, of the term *volume*, and of the term *pressure*, we are certain that we are expressing a necessary law when we say that within certain limits the volume of a gas is inversely proportional to its pressure. A gas would not be a gas if this were not as it is. What will actually happen? Here, again, it must be said that, without further data, we do not know. The behavior predicted by the law of inverse proportion between volume and pressure can fail to be produced. It will not be produced if the temperature varies. We have purposely employed an incomplete formulation of Boyle's Law. "Provided that the temperature remains constant" should be added. But the temperatures may change. The law does not conjecture as to fact; it announces only a *de jure* necessity. The coincidence of the fact and the law depends upon circumstances which no essential determination guarantees.

If to the progress of humanity one attributes a *de jure*

necessity without attributing to it any *de facto* necessity, one protects oneself from any denial arising from the facts of immobility and decadence. Thus understood, the necessity of progress does not imply its inevitability.

Finally, by saying that progress is a necessary thing, one can mean that it is necessary as a factual development. One then affirms that no contingency and no liberty can arrest it. This position has no foundation in a rational analysis of human nature, which reveals only possibilities of progress and exigencies for progress. It does violence to experience. It supposes a quasi-theological concept of the government of history, for which neither historical knowledge nor philosophy affords the least shred of justification. It is the affair of a faith whose motives of credibility are, in the last analysis, purely pragmatic. Progress as a mere possibility and exigency is in no way a substitute for paradise; on the contrary, belief in a factually determined progress, destined to become a reality *no matter what happens*, can be nothing but a substitute for belief in paradise.

The philosophy of necessary progress, announced by the theorists of the eighteenth century and accepted as a fundamental dogma by the public of the nineteenth, attributes to progress a necessity which is more than an exigency and more than a *de jure* necessity: a *de facto* necessity, an inescapable determination. This is the point that must not be lost sight of when one attempts to comprehend the crisis of the idea of progress in our time and the means of surmounting it. As an effect of the emotional character of the romantic belief in progress, the three forms of necessity which our analysis has distinguished have been so intimately confounded, so indissolubly connected, that in renouncing the most fantastic of them, one at the same time renounced a thoroughly established and highly important truth. When the inevitability of progress, as a result of great disillusionments and great catastrophes, became an object of general derision, the voices which should have been raised to remind us that progress is a necessary exigency of our nature remained silent, or, yielding to the general current, added their contribution to a work of deadly negation.

3. For whoever professes an optimistic concept of human nature, the spectacle of the enormous quantity of moral evil existing in mankind at every period of its history is the most insupportable of objections. The naturalistic optimist is forced, since he cannot deny it completely, to reduce to a minimum the role played by malice. Thereafter, he must either shut himself up in a dream (which it is not always possible to do), or else find a sure and easy means of invalidating the great contradiction which threatens to swallow up his belief each time that he finds himself face to face with the reality of history. So he will do what we are in the habit of doing when we wish to exonerate a person who is dear to us, or to exonerate ourselves, from some undeniable fault: as a safe way to dismiss the accusation of malice, he will accuse ignorance and error. Herein lies a simple explanation of the fact that, despite Rousseau's declarations against the sciences and the arts and despite his quarrels with the Encyclopedists, the stream of Rousseauan naturalism quickly merged with the stream of the Philosophy of Enlightenment.

The path of progress is then clearly indicated; it passes through the intellect. Necessary progress consists above all in the improvement and extension of our knowledge. Every victory over ignorance and error lessens the volume of moral evil: if this were not admitted, the great amount of wickedness in human nature would have to be recognized, and that is what naturalistic optimism cannot permit itself to do. It is perfectly logical that the manual of the believers in progress was a work devoted to the advance of human knowledge,

Condorcet's celebrated *Outline for a Historical Panorama of the Progress of the Human Mind*. It was no less logical that the most sonorous popularizer of romantic ideas, Victor Hugo, should have delighted his numberless readers by asserting, with a candor which to us today seems incredible, that the real way to put an end to the gangs of criminals is to multiply schools and libraries.

4. In our brief analysis of the various meanings of the idea of necessary progress, we mentioned, as a form intermediate between necessity understood as a simple exigency and necessity understood as a fatal determination of facts, the concept of a *de jure* necessity capable of being neutralized by the contingencies of *de facto* positions. We do not believe that any important theorist stopped at this intermediate concept; all those who were prepared to accept it adopted it only to pass beyond it, and, to their affirmation of a progress *de jure* necessary added their affirmation of a *de facto* necessary progress. Constantly covered up by an ulterior and more radical concept, the intermediate concept has not been the less active. Into the philosophy of progress it introduced an element with incalculable implications: the assimiliation of humanity to a natural being, acting by determinate causality, instead of acting, as free beings act, by a *superdeterminate* causality which excludes both *de jure* necessity and *de facto* necessity. It is this element of the theory to which must be connected the *technological* character spontaneously attributed to necessary progress.

A technique is a practical discipline based upon scientific knowledge of a complex of laws. It is the instrument by which science ensures man's domination over physical nature. It proceeds by employing determinisms of which science has given it the formula. It has no meaning except in relation to determinate causal relations; and these, by a knowledge of their laws, it causes to serve man's ends. It is applicable to man to the extent that the facts which concern man are subject to determinism, and to that extent only. There are, for example, medical and psychological techniques through which man exercises control over the functioning of his organs and his faculties. As to acts proceeding from free will, they constitute a causal system basically distinct from the universe of determinate natures. No deterministic formula can express them or direct them. A free act proceeds, not—as so many people think—from an indeterminate cause, but from a cause endowed with such an excess of determination that its operation is exerted in a dominating indifference in respect to any necessity. Human acts, by virtue of their very essence as voluntary acts, are outside the domain in which deterministic formulas play their double role of interpretation and direction. The mastery of man over human acts can be exerted only through the knowledge of liberty and through the operation of liberty. There is not—there cannot be—a technique of human acts. A social engineer, able to control human phenomena as an electrical engineer controls electrical phenomena, is nothing but a mythological figure in plain clothes.

Now, when the improvements which had arisen in the positive sciences and in techniques conjured up before men's minds the intoxicating perspective of a rapid and unbounded progress of man's dominion over physical nature, the theorists of progress, unconsciously imitated by some of their opponents, could hardly wait to plunge into a fervid orgy of assimilation and generalization. The marvels accomplished by scientific techniques in the order of physical nature would soon be followed by similar marvels in the order of social nature. All that was needed was to fall to and establish the science of society in conformity with what then appeared to be the eternal model of the physical sciences: the Newtonian system.

The ambition to construct a social science which should

permit the realization of a rational society is everywhere present in the great movement of social thought which was born just after the French Revolution and whose influence, in spite of setbacks and surprises, extends to our own times. We find it in such utopians as Fourier, Saint-Simon, and the Saint-Simonists; in Auguste Comte and his disciples; in the orthodox economists, in a moralist like Proudhon, and in a passionate opponent of revolutionary rationalism, the traditionalist de Bonald. It is extremely striking that these men, despite their divergencies, employ identical expressions upon the subject of a social science: "a rigorous science," "an exact science," "a science as infallible as physics or chemistry," "a science as rigorous as arithmetic or geometry." Each of them dreams of being the Newton of social science, and takes his dream for a reality. Belief in the unity of science dominates the entire picture. It is really less a matter of constructing a social science after the model of the physical sciences than of promoting the development of the one and only science in a field in which it has been held back by particularly tenacious prejudices. As Michelet, the vibrant soul of his generation, put it: "Science is a sacred system whose several parts one should tremble to separate. One ought not to say the sciences, but science." This unitary science supposes a single system of causal relations. The universe of freedom is absorbed into the universe of nature; that is the price which the friends of progress paid for the promise of a rational society. By a paradox full of significance, theorists who announce an era of unprecedented freedom link their anticipations to a postulate which suppresses freedom.

Disillusioned Optimists

In the celebrated introduction to his *Reflections on Violence*, Georges Sorel points out that one of the effects of an optimistic culture is to make men's minds incapable of distinguishing between pessimism and the counterfeits of pessimism.

So little are we prepared to understand pessimism, that we generally employ the word quite incorrectly: we call pessimists people who are in reality only disillusioned optimists. When we meet a man who, having been unfortunate in his enterprises, deceived in his most legitimate ambitions, humiliated in his affections, expresses his griefs in the form of a violent revolt against the duplicity of his associates, the stupidity of society, or the blindness of destiny, we are disposed to look upon him as a pessimist; whereas we ought nearly always to regard him as a disheartened optimist who has not had the courage to start afresh, and who is unable to understand why so many misfortunes have befallen him, contrary to what he supposes to be the general law governing the production of happiness.[2]

These lines were written at a time when a confident optimism still prevailed amongst the public. A few years later, the change being favored by bewildering catastrophes, the era of pessimistic rhetoric began. When we came to realize that that rhetoric had contributed towards making new catastrophes inevitable, we asked ourselves (after rereading Sorel) whether the pessimistic rhetoric we had been hearing expressed an authentic pessimism or a disillusioned optimism. Observing the men around us who were taking an ardent part in the chorus of imprecations against the errors of the age, we had no difficulty in convincing ourselves that these negativists, these merciless nihilists, were completely lacking in the serene energy which is characteristic of souls firmly established in a pessimistic concept. We now propose to set forth the result of our observations upon the ideas and sentiments of these disillusioned optimists.[3]

[2] *Reflections on Violence*, pp. 8–9.
[3] The sophists we are describing owe a part of their prestige to their sustaining an apparent resemblance to the great souls in whom

When a man calls attention to himself by the bitterness, the snarling tone, of his criticisms of modern errors, the aberrations of his contemporaries, the stupidity of the majority, the increasingly rapid decadence of our civilizations, it is generally easy to observe that his psychology is dominated by the feeling of a scandalous contrast. If he considers it necessary to talk so much about evil, to say nothing at all about good, and to prophesy a continual increase of the evils he denounces, it is because, somewhere in his mind, he has a model of harmony to which, whether consciously or unconsciously, he compares the disorders revealed by his daily experience. The disillusioned optimist has the greatest interest in fabricating for himself as pure a model of harmony as possible. He would run the risk of inconsistency if the model to which he refers the data of experience were not immeasurably purer than even the best that experience has the slightest chance of showing him. Upon the purity of his model depends the success of his enterprise. No precaution can be neglected.

1. The construction of his harmonious model begins at the stage of his representation of the physical world. It would be incomplete if it were only a matter of a *Lebens*anschauung; it demands a suitable *Welt*anschauung. The disillusioned optimist owes more than he is aware to the school of Rousseau. His childhood was enchanted by primary-school tales about the finality in nature; his wonder was aroused by the marvels of instinct amongst the insects. If he received any

---

the authentic spirit of prophecy dwells. The discourses of the prophetic spirit are directed towards resurrection and joy, not towards nothingness, like those of disillusioned optimism; they abound in terrible condemnations of the present; but these condemnations proceed from a supernatural image of man according to the divine exigencies, not from a flattering fiction.

instruction in philosophy, his understanding of evil in the kingdoms below man does not go beyond a summary interpretation of the Aristotelian propositions which affirm that the events of nature develop successfully in most cases, and that nature is obstructed only in fewer cases. Does the Aristotelian philosophy of nature, reinforced by the authority of St. Thomas Aquinas, justify an optimistic view of the physical world? Here is a question which we may not leave unanswered.

In regard to the problems of causality and finality, the philosophy of Aristotle and of St. Thomas may be described as a doctrine of nature and necessity associated with a doctrine of contingency and chance. This philosophy rejects the concept of absolute contingency; it sets at the beginning of all becoming the determinations of being, the essences, which doubtless do not exist in a necessary manner, but which are necessarily *what* they are, and which in virtue of their identity with themselves necessarily tend to exercise certain activities and to reach certain ends. But within every natural essence there exists a principle of indeterminateness, matter. Contingency is thus introduced into the world of determinate essences. On the other hand, every natural agent, to attain its ends, has need of the positive cooperation of other agents: this positive cooperation is not guaranteed by any law. In fine, a natural agent can be prevented from attaining its perfection by the action of another agent: against such vexatious encounters nature supplies it with but an insufficient protection. To take a simple example: this winged seed borne by the wind will germinate only if it falls upon fertile soil, where it will enjoy the positive cooperation of all the substances necessary to its growth; it will not germinate if it is immediately eaten by a bird; the young plant will not reach the state of being an adult plant unless it receives a certain quantity of light, heat, and humidity, and unless herbivorous animals pass it by without noticing it. Thus the normal processes make up only a part of the real processes. There is no other normal destiny for a seed than to be transformed into an adult plant capable of reproducing itself; but this is an event which sometimes occurs and sometimes does not.

To recognize normal processes, Aristotelianism proposes the criterion of regularity. The privileged condition of combinations which are regularly produced can be explained only by the play of an essential law. Within every regular system of observable forms, reason recognizes the dynamism of an essence, determined to act and react in a regular manner by virtue of the real identity of its natural constitution and its essential tendencies. The ambiguity of the word *regularity* expresses in the happiest manner the connection which reason spontaneously perceives to exist between frequency and law; when one describes an event as regular, one means both that it is frequent and that it is produced in conformity with a rule—that is to say, that it is normal. Reversing the point of view, one can say that the event of nature, having essential necessity on its side, must have frequency on its side, and that the event foreign to natural finalities, being upheld by no rule, can be produced only irregularly, therefore rarely.

Any science of nature presupposes and confirms the truth of these formulas. But it often happens that the exact sense of an incontestably true proposition is extremely difficult to express unequivocally. To our knowledge, the usual expositions of Aristotelianism on the subject of frequency and legality do not have all the definiteness necessary to obviate an ambiguity of great import. If one undiscriminatingly accepts the thesis that the event of nature is actually produced in the majority of cases and that natural finalities are translated into facts by a frequency of successful results, one arrives at an image of the world in which evils appear only rarely. This image is contradicted by innumerable familiar experiences, but that does not much trouble professors of philosophy, amongst whom school adages too often create habits of mind unfavorable to the perception of familiar truths. That a fish egg should become an adult fish conforming to its specific type is a normal and happy event, in which the mind recognizes the successful operation of a natural tendency in motion towards its end. Is this event produced in the majority of cases? A carp lays about three hundred thousand eggs every spring. Fishermen are supposed to consider themselves fortunate if seven or eight of the fry, out of the three hundred thousand, reach adulthood—so great is the menace of insects, amphibia, and carnivorous fishes to immature fish. What is obviously true for fish is true in varying degree for most living species. The victory of natural finalties appears to be a comparatively exceptional outcome, accomplished amongst a multitude of defeats. Sometimes the number of defeats is so great that the entire species disappears.

The optimistic interpretation of the relations between the number of successful instances and the total number of actual instances arises from the fact that not enough attention has been paid to the consequences of the multiplicity of species and of the conflict between their goods. For if it is normal for a seed to be transformed into a plant, and for a small fish to grow large, it is not less normal for a granivorous bird to feed on seeds and for a carnivorous fish to eat small fish. Consequently, to define the frequency of the normal event, transformation of seed into plant, it is necessary to include in the computation the frequency of another normal event, which is the food consumption of granivora; to define the frequency of the normal event, growth of a small fish, it is necessary to include in the computation another normal event, the food consumption of carnivora. These brief indications suffice to show that the very real connection between finality and frequency nowise justifies the opinion that in each of the species below the human kingdom good occurs more frequently than evil.[4]

Once these things are comprehended, the notions of nature, determinism, finality, regularity retain all their meaning. But the vision of a physical world in which evil plays but a small part and does not trouble the observer's serenity is thenceforth impossible. Such an idyllic view is so contrary to experience that it could never have been maintained if it were not marvelously in harmony with a certain moral attitude. Here is a true story which briefly epitomizes the whole question.

A theologian had just learned that the wife of a friend of his was suffering from postpuerperal phlebitis. Though he expressed his sympathy, he did not fail to remark that the misfortune was a consequence of original sin. A critically minded philosopher who overheard his remarks pointed out that if phlebitis amongst young mothers is a consequence, it is not a formal consequence, of original sin. The philosopher knew rural life as the theologian did not know it. He went on to point out that delivering a cow is always a delicate operation and that accidents in giving birth are not rare in the bovine species. The theologian looked startled; a portion of his vision of the world had tottered. He exclaimed: "Isn't that a result of domestication?" There are no statistics on puerperal accidents amongst wild cattle; but the interesting thing is the theologian's postulate. He simply postulated that streptococci have no right to establish themselves in organisms enfeebled

[4] St. Thomas expressly states that the human species is the only one in which evil occurs more frequently than good. But this formulation appears in contexts which narrowly limit its meaning: it is concerned only with the inner relation of an act to its end and does not imply necessarily any conjecture as to what occurs when the action of an agent demands the cooperation of other agents or is exposed to the contrary action of other agents. On the other hand, it should probably be confessed that the *cosmic image* of St. Thomas retains an optimistic coloring, apparently of Greek origin.

by maternity so long as man does not come with his sin to disturb the course of nature's harmonies. Though the reader may have thought otherwise, the theologian in question was a man of powerful intellect; but, in several respects, he was a quite typical example of the disillusioned optimist.

This, then, we must hold for certain: far from suggesting the idea of an order established at small cost, in contrast to the high cost of order in the human species, physical nature presents us with the spectacle of an order which contains a ceaseless struggle and immense destruction. The idyllic picture of the physical world is the product of a predetermined moral attitude. The true cosmic picture can suggest only pessimism—but a confident pessimism, since it reveals that, through all conflicts and sacrifices, nature still finds means to convey to our minds the mystery of divine wisdom and of impassive love.

2. The model of harmony supplied by a sophistic interpretation of physical nature has only a distant connection with the problems of action. Its importance arises from its comprehensiveness and from the depth of the level at which it is seated. As thought approaches action, new models of harmony appear, rendering more and more intense the contrast in which the disillusioned optimist finds justification for his imprecations and negations.

The next stage consists in a particular version (entirely implicit in many cases) of the dogmas which concern the original innocence and the fall of man. Confining ourselves to repeating what we have learned from the most trustworthy theologians, we may say that the state of original innocence is defined by a system of preternatural and supernatural gifts which protect man from the miseries of his condition and raise him, in the order of the knowledge and love of God, to a condition which no created or creatable being can reach by the unaided forces of its nature. Original sin brought about the loss of these superadded gifts. But in stripping off its gratuitous gifts, nature received wounds. The man of original sin is not only a stripped man (*homo nudatus*), he is a wounded man (*homo vulneratus*). Thus, original sin has two kinds of consequences. Its formal consequences are the wounds of sin, the troublesome dispositions, the radical incapacities, whose proper cause is sin and which would not have existed if man had been created in the state of pure nature. Its material consequences consist in the re-establishment of conditions natural to man, conditions whose proper cause is human nature and of which original sin is the cause only in a historical sense. Death, disease, irksomeness of labor, are material consequences of original sin. If man had been created in the state of pure nature, he would have known death, he would have been subject to disease, constrained to painful work, and exposed to many other rigors and miseries.

Any attempt to minimize the consequences of original sin is impious. But neither is it a work of piety to transform the merely material consequences of original sin into formal consequences. So doing, one surreptitiously arrives at regarding the preternatural and supernatural gifts of the state of innocence as properties of human nature, which is philosophically and theologically absurd. This error, at least in its milder forms, is extremely current, both amongst the generality of believers and amongst those religious thinkers who lack that sense of the relations between nature and the supernatural (substantial or modal) which is the glory of the school of St. Thomas.

Not enough attention has been given to the importance of the role played in the construction of Pascal's pessimism by the extremely optimistic idea he entertains of uncorrupted human nature. "In many cases in which Pascal indignantly says 'corrupted nature,' he [St. Thomas] teaches us to say

often with compassion, 'human nature.' " [5] Because of his exalted views of uncorrupted nature, Pascal attributes to the
corruption of sin a number of characteristics which really result from the constitution of our nature. The extremeness of
his judgments upon the corruption of nature is connected
with an extreme estimate of the natural possibilities of man.
The effect of contrast is powerful, and largely contributes to
explain Pascal's skepticism towards law, his painful cynicism
in respect to natural equity and to justice in temporal societies. For Pascal, as for Rousseau, there is "no justice in
the human city as time has little by little constituted it." [6]
Whereupon, Rousseau recommends a revolt against the creations of time; Pascal, submission to the order established by
force. By reducing the effect of contrast through an authentically pessimistic estimate of our human condition, one perceives that justice is not entirely absent from temporal history, despite the wounds of sin. Then one understands that
the struggle for justice is not doomed to certain defeat, that it
is not absolutely impossible to cause what is just to be also
strong—it is only extremely difficult. The triumph of justice
is not without precedent in our history, and if it is not for us
to establish a perfect and unshakable justice, it is our responsibility to multiply the triumphs of the imperfect and precarious justice which is well worth our dying for it. True pessimism restores confidence and frees energies stupefied by the
contrasts which are kept alive by attachment to a model
created by an optimistic imagination.

When one descends from the sublime reaches of Pascal's
thought to the level of weak souls subject to considerations of
self-interest, the harmonious model afforded by an exalted
concept of human nature without original sin no longer suf-

[5] J. Maritain, *Réflexions sur l'intelligence*, 1st ed. (Paris: Desclée,
1931?), p. 334.
[6] *Ibid.*, p. 63.

fices. Original sin, if it is sincerely conceived, has the serious disadvantage of affecting the whole of humanity—myself and my friends as well as our opponents. It is therefore necessary to construct a model of harmony which can be recognized in some definite part of humanity. With a little cleverness, we shall doubtless succeed in getting ourselves a place amongst the harmonious part of our species. From that privileged position we shall be able to secure ourselves all kinds of advantages (particularly moral ones) by tirelessly denouncing the rule of evil in the part of humanity in which we shall have been careful not to place ourselves.

3. The first phase of this decisive operation consists in constructing a retrospective utopia. Whereas the confident optimist puts his utopia in the future, the disillusioned optimist puts his in the past. In a sense, this is much safer. For as time passes, the future becomes the present and pictures of the future become susceptible to verification in immediate experience—a misfortune which nowise threatens fictions safely placed in the past.

It has often been observed that confident optimism, particularly when it takes the form of a philosophy of necessary progress, creates dispositions unfavorable to passionate action. Why go to so much trouble to bring about a better world, if progress is brought about by the force of events, regardless of our personal lassitude, our personal desertion? The fatalism of progress, like all fatalisms, indubitably tends to produce an arrest of life. It is particularly in the order of common moral beliefs, and of the institutions which are related to those beliefs, that the fatalism of progress seems actually to have favored an attitude of passivity before evil. As an example, let us cite the evolution of the ideas, habits, and laws relative to marriage in the western world as a whole, from the end of the eighteenth century to our own time. This evolution, on the whole a great process of decadence, has been astonishingly general, profound, and tenacious. It is easy to understand what its promoters sought from this evolution. But it has been tolerated, accepted resignedly and unresistingly, by many who in no way approved of the growing lack of discipline in morals. This was because people saw in it an inevitable development, connected with other aspects of the evolution of modern societies, inseparable from what it had been agreed to call progress, and consequently mysteriously oriented towards a better state of things.

These remarks will suffice to show that we are not at all inclined to underestimate the stultifying effects which confident optimism is likely to produce. It must, however, be remarked that in numerous fields—such as scientific research, industrial activities, public education, social medicine, administration, colonization, and so forth—confident optimism has often played the role of a stimulus to action. Whatever their philosophic professions may have been, men of action faced with their tasks did not take the dogma of the inevitability of progress too seriously.

Disillusioned optimism, on the other hand, with its retrospective utopias, produces an extraordinary torpor in the most varied fields. Of all fatalisms, that which most surely kills action is the fatalism which refuses any place in the future to the vision of a better world and puts it back in the past—in a past which grows more distant every day. Reflecting upon the great fall of the French nation, on the bewildering succession of defeats of which the military defeat of 1940 was the terrible end (soon followed by symptoms of a rebirth), seeking desperately to assign causes to it, we became convinced that all the assignable causes were reducible to an immense and mysterious *privation* which could only be described, despite the vagueness of the phrase, as a *general lack of vitality* affecting particularly the governing classes. But this deep and central cause itself demands explanation. How, then, had the governing classes, but lately so intrepid, come to put security first of all things, and to renounce greatness? To give a satisfactory answer to this question, it would doubtless be necessary to invoke a large number of factors, both economic and ideological or moral, and to estimate their relations. First place amongst the ideological factors we should give to the astounding success of restrospective utopias amongst the last generation of the Third Republic.

Even if they belonged to the conservative section of the nation, which had never wholeheartedly accepted the most definitive conquests of the Revolution, our fathers had been educated in a concept of history which pictured the past under clouds and darkness. Aware of the exaggerations in Michelet's awe-inspiring descriptions, they continued to believe in *lettres de cachet*, in underground dungeons, in the Massacre of St. Bartholomew; they still believed that the finances of the Monarchy were in a deplorable state on the eve of the Revolution, that the eighteenth-century nobility was profoundly corrupt, that Louis XV was guilty of the gravest prevarications; they still believed that the Middle Ages were a period when slaughter and pillage ran rife, that the Hundred Years' War, for example, had been a pretty sinister affair, that the condition of the serfs was not to be envied, and that it was good to have been born into a century in which famine and pestilence had become rather rare. A century earlier, the first generation of Romantics had popularized the picture of a Middle Ages which was all chivalry, humanity, organic solidarity, vocational conscience, protection of widows and orphans, courtly love, and poetry; but everyone had understood that this was but literary entertainment.

Immediately after the First World War, the fashionable pictures of the old regime and the Middle Ages underwent a radical change. Many historians and dabblers in history undertook to avenge the past upon its calumniators. They were playing an easy game, for the Revolutionary writers had successfully popularized a number of sinister fables on the subject of earlier societies; what was more serious, they had shown themselves incapable of understanding the real merits of those societies. The new fashion reaped the benefit of a needed reaction. But the needed reaction was soon overstepped, and under pressure from political and ideological passions the Middle Ages of the first-generation Romantics established itself imperturbably in all kinds of supposedly scientific publications. A considerable portion of the public welcomed these new versions, being delighted to find its revenge in their optimistic picture of the past. For there was a need of revenge for the confidence with which men had received the promises of the philosophy of progress and the bitter disillusionments which had ensued. Belief in necessary progress was dead. It had been replaced by a sort of satanic myth of necessary decadence. Soon the stampede was general: all that mattered was to find a refuge from the call of an action doomed to defeat from the first and even, perhaps, condemned to precipitate the inevitable increase of evil. Each found a refuge according to his taste—in pleasure, in a quiet, unpretentious life, in esthetic refinement, in speculative studies, and even in higher activities. It is not at all certain that the most pernicious abstentions should be laid to those who took refuge in pleasure.

4. By damning the present and the future for the benefit of a utopia set up in the past, does one not condemn oneself? Not necessarily. Actually, it is easy to imagine that we—my friends and myself and those who think as we do—represent a privileged survival from a happier age, a species invulnerable to the deluge of corruption which has not ceased to rain down upon the world ever since the uncertain origin of modern times. Thus is continuity established between the harmonious

model set up in the past and the one which the disillusioned optimist seldom fails to set up in the present. Here indeed is the last, and the most immediately effective, of the contrasts which nourish the false pessimist's imprecations: the contrast between the ignorance, the stupidity, the improvidence, the brutality, the bad manners of the common run of mankind, and the wisdom, the prudence, the justice of a relatively small group, called the upper class, the governing class, the elite, high society, sometimes simply *society*—as if those who did not belong to it were outside of society.

In earlier days the governing class was defined by titles transmissible by inheritance, together with property in land, certain social functions, and certain legal privileges. In the course of the nineteenth century, the rich bourgeoisie largely took over the succession of the nobility, and for several generations the governing class was chiefly defined by the possession of capital. Today, as a result of the impoverishment of considerable sections of the bourgeoisie and the old nobility, it has become extremely difficult to say what token it is that confers upon an individual the quality of being a member of the upper class. The truth seems to be that this quality is determined by several tokens, which to a certain extent replace one another when they are not united, and which reinforce one another when they are united. The chief of these tokens are wealth, the exercise of functions of command and, more generally, of highly esteemed functions; the fact of belonging to a family known to have exercised such functions; and, to a lesser degree, learning and culture. The upper class in modern nations mimics aristocracy and values lineage: however, it is prepared to confer the highest positions upon men of modest or even plebeian origin, provided that they have proved their complete incorporation into the upper class by their sentiments and their conduct.

Fascism and more especially Nazism often had recourse to the revolt of the masses against the domination of the governing classes. With the decline of these movements, it is probable that opposition to democracy (I mean overt opposition) will again for a time become the monopoly of parties and persons who intended to leave or to restore the direction of public affairs—with all the advantages and prerogatives attached to it—to a minority constituted, maintained, and recruited in a manner that makes it possible to elude public supervision.

Upon the role of the governing classes in a democracy much could be said. It would be profitable, in particular, to undertake an extremely careful examination of the relations which the concept of a governing class has on the one hand with the system of classes resulting from capitalist organization and, on the other hand, with the eternal necessities of a hierarchic differentiation of society. Whatever may be the answer to these problems, which are foreign to the aim of this study, it may be said without temerity that the mystical or mythological factor which has so greatly contributed to maintain actually aristocratic regimes under the forms of democracy was very rudely handled by the experiences of the last few years. After having witnessed, with an extraordinary poisoning of evidence, to what lengths ignorance, naïveté, incompetence, stupidity, the cruel egotism and the felony of our betters can go, our contemporaries will be little disposed to become excited over the contrast—dear to all aristocracies—between the wisdom of the governing classes and the folly of the people. The groups whose function it is to preserve the ideas of authority and hierarchy will do well to resign themselves to this fact and to give up compromising those ideas by a selective optimism which is condemned by facts too serious, too numerous, and too obvious to be soon forgotten.

The catastrophes of our epoch have taught us to extend our pessimism to all periods of history and to all sections of society.

A Pessimistic Theory of Progress

The theory of progress has been so generally associated with optimistic concepts that it is paradoxical to speak of a theory of progress constructed within the framework of a pessimistic philosophy. But once one has understood that the criticism of the idea of progress which was current during the last generation proceeds from a kind of optimism rather than from true pessimism, the paradox ceases to be troubling.

The pessimism which we recommend is in no sense a metaphysical theory; it is a point of view upon moral reality and upon history, not a theory of being. In metaphysics, the fundamental truths are optimistic propositions; the pessimistic propositions express only subordinate truths, conditioned truths, circumscribed truths. Every being is good, existence is good, the Supreme Being is Supreme Goodness—these propositions absolutely exclude any pessimistic position which should claim, on any grounds whatever, to assume the value of an ultimate truth. By attributing to evil the character of a positive reality, by imagining a principle of evil capable of neutralizing the principle of good, the Manichaeism of all ages commits precisely the error of erecting pessimistic propositions into ultimate truths, equal in dignity to propositions which relate to the good. Thereby, Manichaeism is obliged to corrupt whatever it touches. Let us beware lest it corrupt moral pessimism.

In a general way, any conception of life whose center is the exaltation of an insoluble antithesis or of a conflict without issue may be described as a moral pessimism perverted by a metaphysical error. Sometimes the conflict is between good and evil; in that case, if it is held to be insoluble, it is because one has lost sight of the absolute sovereignty of good. Sometimes the conflict is between two forces equally devoted to good; but then, if it is held to be insoluble, it is because one imagines, within the good, a basic division, an ultimate contradiction, by ignoring the perfect unity, the peace, the joy which are the attributes of Supreme Goodness. Undoubtedly any philosophy of tragic heroism must be said to imply the exalting but finally ruinous fiction of a division affecting good at its inmost source. The most typical and most successful of the Greek tragedies have their motive force in a conflict which is pursued even into the absolute. *Oedipus the King* is a duel between a good man and destiny. The tragedy does not accuse Oedipus, the involuntary murderer of his father, the involuntary husband of his mother, the benefactor of a city, the father of a people; nor does it accuse destiny, which punishes a good man for the crimes he has committed involuntarily, under the influence of destiny. Oedipus is a criminal and is not a criminal: his story seems to signify that peace is not promised to men of good will.

All that is essentially implied by moral pessimism is a profound feeling of the wretchedness of our condition; a perfectly sincere disposition to see evil wherever it shows itself, together with its frequency and its extent; will and resolution to knock down the protective screens which our fear and our laziness manufacture to spare us the sight of evil; a thorough sense of the immense difficulties which the accomplishment of good presents. One could say that pessimism is nothing but *depth of moral intelligence.* In the life of study, what distinguishes really intelligent people from those who have only a brilliant appearance of intelligence is an ability to understand that the most trifling questions, once examined, will always turn out to be incomparably more difficult than one could have foreseen, to understand that any progress in the exploration of a question necessarily has the effect of making new difficulties apparent, difficulties greater than those already surmounted. Only shallow minds believe that there are such things as easy questions in the sciences, in philosophy and history. Profound minds know that there are no easy questions. Yet they are not morose minds; they have accepted the law of difficulty which is the law of our intelligence; and to the cheap satisfactions obtained by brilliant and shallow minds they prefer the austere joys which accompany familiarity with mystery. Optimists are men who believe that there are easy questions in the order of human action; men who believe that one can easily be good, become better, improve mankind's lot: they are the shallow minds, the idiots, of the moral order.

Just as a profound scientific mind is not necessarily a morose mind, so a pessimist has no reason to be a sullen person. It is the disillusioned optimist who has good reasons for losing sight of the possibility of progress and the exigency for progress which are written in our nature: for him the practical solution is to let things go. But to the true pessimist this is an inadmissible solution: an exact knowledge of evil reveals the power of good and arouses in our souls an uncompromising will to act and to struggle for the better world whose realization our nature, from the depths of its wretchedness, demands.

If it is true that the necessity of progress is reducible to the necessity of a possibility and of an exigency, no a priori statement can provide the least element of an answer to the question, *What of progress as a fact?* This question is referable entirely to experience. To propound it correctly, it is indispensable to take into consideration the indubitably narrow limits of the comparative investigations which have some likelihood of reaching a soundly based answer. Bearing in mind these limits, we propose the following methodological rules: (1) Give up propounding the question of *de facto* progress in terms which embrace the whole complex of human activities. Let any question concerning the fact of progress be relative to a well-defined order of activity, such as positive science, techniques, the fine arts, relations under the civil law, etc. (2) Let any question concerning the fact of progress mention the period during which we wish to know whether progress has been made; let all such questions cease to refer to the whole of humanity; let them define the particular societies to which they are intended to refer.

Applying these rules, we shall not be afraid to declare that the western world has made undoubted progress in the domain of positive science, in the domain of technique, in the domain of the moral conscience, throughout the period which extends from the Renaissance to our own days. It would be possible to demonstrate other facts of progress in the same societies during the same epoch of history. To simplify matters we shall abstain from exploring them.

No one will contest the progress of the positive and technical sciences. But many moralists deny that this progress has the nature of a true progress for mankind; they maintain that scientific and technical development has produced more disastrous results than real improvements, so that, considering the total effect, far more evil has been done than good. But since no one sincerely believes that it is possible to arrest or even to retard the progress of sciences and techniques, condemnation of their progress is invariably accompanied by a fatalism of decadence. Few problems are so important for the morality of modern times as the problem of the attitude to adopt towards the irrepressible fecundity of the scientific and technical intellect. This attitude must be unmistakably defined; it is therefore necessary to attempt to establish principles which will make it possible to eliminate the confusion prevailing in discussions of the problem.

1. Scientific and technical progress would not be the object of so much vituperation if we had not behind us the great illusion (cultivated by the Philosophy of Enlightenment, by Romanticism, and by scientism) that the proper effect of the perfections of the theoretic or demiurgic intellect is to make men better *absolutely speaking*. Repeatedly denounced, repeatedly execrated, this illusion still remains active and formidable in the back of our minds—otherwise we should not feel the need to assail it with new denunciations and new execrations. Current criticism of scientific and technical progress expends a great deal of energy in setting forth considerations which amount to saying that science and technique lend themselves indifferently to the service of good and the service of evil. One fails to observe that, by making so much noise over a self-evident and easily comprehended proposition, one ends by obscuring its obviousness in the eyes of a good many people. It is virtue alone that can be put to no bad use. It is to virtue, not to science or technique, that it falls to make men good, absolutely speaking. It is highly regrettable that such truths are not clear to everyone. But there are great disadvantages in letting the length of our discourses and the heat of our rhetoric lead people to believe that it could ever have been reasonable to expect science or technique to provide any guarantee of right use.

2. Once the false problem has been eliminated root and branch, the true problem propounds itself of itself. Any increase of a power susceptible to misuse is likely to be translated into facts by increasing evils. All would be well if virtue increased in the same proportion as the power. But the pessimistic concept which we have been at pains to set forth makes us fear that such is not the case. So it signifies little whether science and technique are things good in themselves;

handled by evil wills, their progress will serve but to increase the sum of human ills.

Probable as this line of reasoning may appear, its conclusion can be verified only by experience. But in the extremely arduous operation of verifying it, predetermined moral attitudes, esthetic tastes, the usual views of the physiognomy of historical periods, almost always play the role of disturbing factors so radically that, instead of a verification, what we obtain is a brief, whose interest (if it have any) is but that of revealing its author's personality.

To improve the state of the question, it would be of great value to establish a complete list of the prejudices which are most frequently at work in the judgments of our contemporaries upon the actual results of scientific and technical progress in terms of human happiness. Merely as a suggestion, let us point out the disastrous influence of retrospective utopias, the tendency to accord more attention to clamorous and sensational evils than to goods which are concealed by their very familiarity; and there is also the particular mythology of culture manufactured in our own day by idle writers which classes as "materialism" any activity whose proper effect is to feed the hungry and relieve the afflicted. Let us boldly declare our conviction that an unprejudiced inquiry would reach the conclusion that, despite the frequency of misuse, science and technique have contributed much towards the good of humanity in the limited realm in which it falls to them to better the condition of men.

3. Furthermore, about what are we arguing? We are committed. It is claimed that the artisans of Greece, who were able to create machines and who knew it, voluntarily restrained their inventive genius for fear of increasing the destructive power of evil wills. Even were it proper to conclude

—as we are nowise inclined to do—that it is regrettable that modern man should have abandoned this attitude of prudent suspicion, one must still resign oneself to the fact that modern man has abandoned it. The creation of a progressive technical environment is the most obvious example of an irrevocable decision that can possibly be found in human history. Fundamentally, everyone is here in agreement. Plans for a return to a primitive technical environment are the dreams of amateurs whom no one takes seriously. The whole of the real problem is to recognize and to further those economic, political, and social institutions which promote the right use of techniques by directing their power towards satisfying man's true needs. It is here, doubtless, that the shoe pinches us—for the institutions which are favorable to a right use of techniques are those which distribute the power they give, which divide it by putting it at everyone's service. In the matter of applied chemistry, for example, the average man is less interested in poison gases than in complete foods, effectual medicines, and windows which transmit ultraviolet rays. But by distributing the power of techniques to the average man, one is likely to increase the power of the average man—and there are those who disapprove of that.

The Evolution of Conscience

As regards the moral order itself, we shall set aside as too ambitious, or at least as too complex, all questions which imply a comparison between the total amounts of good and evil which exist in humanity, or even in a definite fraction of humanity, at two epochs of its history. Many people do not hesitate to assert that men were better a century ago than they are today. A small number of confident optimists—the species has become rare nowadays—will, with no less assurance, assert that we are, on the whole, better than our forefathers. But is it possible to define a method which will permit one to verify these mass hypotheses? We shall abstain from passing judgment upon this question. What we propose to do is but to consider the evolution of a factor in general morality, to wit, the knowledge of good and evil, the moral conscience. But to increase our chances of arriving at a sound solution, we shall limit our inquiry to the chosen few, to those persons who, at any given moment of history, represent the highest degree of moral perfection attained by humanity. It is comparatively easy to know what ideas the most just men of our time entertain on the subject of good and evil. On the other hand, numerous documents permit one to construct a reasonably clear picture of the moral conscience of a man of the thirteenth century or of the Renaissance. Thus the comparison is based upon precise data. There is no doubt about the nature of the answer: an examination of the moral conscience of just men during the last few centuries of the history of our societies reveals great progress. It does not follow that the world is better, absolutely speaking; it does not follow that today's saints are greater saints than the saints of old. It follows only that morality has risen to a higher *state* in the persons of its most perfect representatives. And this is not a negligible result.[7]

We shall take our examples from the order of the virtue of justice (in the proper sense), for it is there chiefly that remarkable progress has been made.

1. In the Middle Ages, and even in modern times at a not very distant period, the most honest consciences—to say nothing of the remainder—universally admitted that any man taking part in an unjust war was personally culpable and con-

---

[7] On the progressive character of the moral conscience, *cf.* J. Maritain, *La conscience morale et l'état de nature* (New York: Editions de La Maison Française, 1942).

sequently liable to personal punishment. The prisoner of war, recently involved in an unjust action, should consider himself fortunate if he were reduced to slavery: to make him a slave was to remit the death penalty which he had deserved, *servus, servatus*. Upon which, it was enough to suppose that the Negroes captured by African coast kinglets had been made prisoners by just belligerents, and the slavers' consciences were clear.

We have learned to make a distinction between individual guilt and collective guilt. We have come to understand that a soldier taken prisoner by a just belligerent becomes—immediately, and by the very fact that he ceases to be engaged in an unjust collective action—a person enjoying the same presumption of innocence as any one of our own fellow citizens. To kill him would be as great a crime as any ordinary murder; to make him a slave would be as abominable as to send any harmless and peaceable citizen to the galleys. To ill-treat him, to feed him inadequately, to lodge him inadequately, to force him to work beyond his strength, are iniquities. The just belligerent has no right except that of preventing a prisoner from returning to an unjust collective action by escaping. If the camp guards fire on an escaping prisoner, well and good; by crossing the boundary of the camp, he again becomes what he had lately been—an unjust belligerent. As long as he submits to remaining a prisoner—that is to say, a nonbelligerent—he has an absolute right to the treatment that we should desire for one of our brothers if he should be taken prisoner.

2. Another particularly striking example concerns the problem of destitution. Not for long have all just men regarded destitution as a social iniquity. I am speaking of destitution, not of poverty, and of destitution amongst decent people, not of the destitution to which gamblers, alcoholics, debauchees,

and idlers condemn themselves. Until a comparatively recent period, then, everyone (just men not excepted) held that the destitution of the working classes was justified by a social necessity. The reasoning was as follows: Every society requires so large an amount of manual labor that it can be supplied only by a great number of men; the working class will be the most numerous class. Now, manual labor is such a painful thing that the only way to make men consent to perform it is to let them feel the spur of destitution. Without that spur, who would be willing to plow the earth, to risk being caught in a mine explosion or a shipwreck? Eliminate destitution, and no one would be willing to work.

We have come to understand that, given certain technical improvements in combination with certain economic and social improvements, a workman who earns ten or twelve dollars a day can work with a zeal incomparably greater than that which was brought to their tasks by the destitute of old. Is not this outlawing of destitution by the consciences of just men an incontestable step forward, and a thousand times more important than the most obvious examples of progress in techniques?

3. Principles relative to the justice of war were formulated with great clarity as far back as the Middle Ages; but as regards their application to actual political and military situations, the consciences of just men have but recently been awakened. As James T. Shotwell remarks, "prior to 1914 war was regarded as a legitimate instrument of policy which could be used by a sovereign state whenever its government deemed it necessary." [8] The idea of applying to the decisions of a sovereign state the criteria of justice defined by theologians and philosophers had hardly been born. Now, experience

[8] James T. Shotwell, *What Germany Forgot* (New York: Macmillan, 1940), p. 97.

bears witness that in our epoch, so fruitful in crimes, criminals can no longer count on finding just men's consciences asleep; just men's consciences are sensitive to crimes which not long ago left them indifferent. The history of the reactions provoked throughout the world by the Italian campaign in Ethiopia is particularly significant in this regard. There were some who, without contesting the injustice of the Italian enterprise, asked us if it was really opportune, in connection with this expedition, to raise a question of conscience which had not been raised in connection with other colonial conquests apparently no less unjust. Thus, because the moral conscience of just men had often shown itself indifferent to the crimes of the past, it ought to have remained indifferent to the crimes of the present. The poor fellows who reasoned in this fashion ignored both the need of progress which is written in our nature and the fact of the progress recently accomplished by the moral conscience of just men in discerning certain concrete goods and certain concrete evils.

In our examination of the facts of scientific and technical progress, our remarks related to the whole of a society, or rather of a group of societies. In our examination of the progress of the moral conscience, our remarks related to a small number of privileged souls. This difference in method was imposed upon us by differences in the manner in which the facts of progress became part of the social patrimony and are preserved from generation to generation.

What happens in the realm of the positive sciences? Scientific discoveries, made public by reports to learned societies, by educational institutions, by periodicals and books, usually obtain general acceptance after a period of discussion which is necessary to test their truth. The worst that can happen is that prejudice may prolong this probationary period beyond what is strictly required by a due regard for the proper establishment of truth. Once general acceptance is secured, the newly discovered truth acquires a definite sociological existence, it becomes part of the transmissible common good of humanity. The operation has been accomplished by the spontaneous play of social relations, without the necessity of any intervention on the part of the conscious centers of society. Or, if they have intervened, they have played only a subordinate role—for example, as a timely stimulus (by awarding a scientist honors which will attract attention to his work), or as an official consecration of the spontaneous agreement of thinking minds (by including a newly accepted theory in scholastic programs).

It is in the same fashion that technical improvements acquire a sociological existence and remain in possession of it. In this realm, even more than in the realm of positive speculation, ease of communications guarantees that beneficial novelties will be incorporated into the common patrimony by spontaneous socialization. Pasteur's work on the etiological role of microorganisms aroused passionate opposition; but it was inevitable that the opposition should soon be overcome by the power of an easily communicable truth. The principles of surgical asepsis quickly forced their own acceptance through their brilliant results. The conscious centers of society intervened only after the battle had been won, to give the new techniques the supplementary guarantee of legal sanctions.

Let us now consider this progress in the moral order, whose essence, in the terms of our analysis, is an increase in the light which the moral conscience can bring to bear upon its effort to distinguish good from evil. It is supremely important to determine exactly the conditions which permit newly established moral truths to acquire sociological existence, to grow in it, and to conserve the qualitative and quantitative positions they have gained there.

The discovery of moral truth is generally an obscure, anonymous, secret thing. It is the work of an unorganized group of persons who do not know one another and who pursue their researches in solitude. No one can assign it a date; all that chronologists can say is that, at a certain period in history, a certain moral truth passed beyond the phase of individual adherences; it appears in letters, memoirs, literary work, it is talked about, attacked and defended, it circulates—in a word, it has acquired a sociological existence. Then a day comes, perhaps after a long period of waiting, when the new idea is embodied in a deathless work—the writings of a great thinker, or the career of a hero. Thereafter its sociological existence is definitively consolidated. Happen what may, the idea will never disappear from history.

Up to this point, the conscious centers of society have had no occasion to intervene; if they have intervened, it is accidentally, and their intervention is likely to have been unfortunate. But the result, actually achieved at this moment of the process, remains far below what the service of man demands. What remains to be accomplished is that the moral truth which has been newly recognized by a few privileged souls should enlighten other souls, that it should be placed within reach of all sincere minds, that it should win over the greatest possible number of consciences, that it should take its place amongst the principles which a morally normal man will never openly call into question. If it happens that this *distribution* of moral truth does not take place, the progress accomplished by the elect in the realm of the moral conscience will have suffered a disaster. It is as if a handful of biologists, convinced by Pasteur, had found themselves powerless to convince surgeons, midwives, and mothers of the necessity for asepsis. Surgical and obstetrical massacres and infant mortality would not appreciably have diminished.

We need to ask ourselves if the diffusion of moral truth is brought about in the same way as the diffusion of scientific and technical truth—that is to say, through spontaneous social relations. Let us be careful to note that the thing which guarantees the spontaneous diffusion of scientific and technical truth is its property of easily imposing itself upon the majority of minds. If moral truth has the same property, its diffusion will be normally assured without any necessity for intervention on the part of the conscious centers of society. Has moral truth the property of easily imposing itself upon the majority of minds? Is it true that it is easily communicable? On the contrary, must it not be said that the strength of collective habits, of the impulses and the inhibitions which arise from familiar images, the silent seductions of inertia, the passions, and above all the agony which takes possession of the conscience when, under an increase of light, certain acts which have habitually been performed without remorse are likely to seem criminal—must it not be said that all these causes for blindness have a most terrible likelihood of prevailing over a newly discovered moral truth, of arresting its progress as soon as it tries to expand its sociological existence beyond the limits of a small group of particularly pure consciences?

To keep the struggle from being too unequal, the conscious centers of society must pronounce in favor of the new idea and ensure its distribution, as well as its preservation, by putting at its service the unequaled pedagogical force constituted by the machinery of positive law. Only then will the difficulties which oppose the communication of moral truth cease to be insurmountable. By being incorporated into legal practice, moral truth penetrates into the very citadel of ignorance and error, into that obscure realm of familiar, tenacious, and dominating images, the purification of which is the absolute condition of lucidity of conscience.

Let us take an example drawn from contemporary history in the field of labor relations. In our time, what would be the reaction of an industrialist if someone should propose to him that he make children work twelve hours a day in unhealthy workshops? We assume that the industrialist in question is an ordinary man, neither more nor less enlightened than the people around him—one who insists that honesty is still the best policy, a decent man, incapable of heroism. The proposal will arouse him to sincere indignation: he will swear that he would rather turn beggar than become a torturer of children.

Let us now reflect upon the conditions under which children worked in the factories of only a century ago. Let us re-read the reports of Buret, of Villermé, of Engels. Did employers in those days have the souls of criminals? We have every reason to believe that many of them were very worthy men, as lacking in bloodthirstiness as in heroic virtues. They were good husbands and excellent fathers, they were generous to their old servants (those who had survived), and gave a good deal of money to charities. As for the lives, as for the souls, of the children whom their machines consumed at such a horrible rate—on that subject their consciences said nothing whatever; their consciences were reduced to silence by a system of protective images called "the inescapable laws of economic life," "painful necessities," "the natural order," "the necessary organization of society," and so forth. When the conscious centers of society decided—oh, so gradually and timidly!—to introduce the protest of justice into positive law, great was the general indignation. Had not the natural order been sacrilegiously attacked? A century has passed, and the laws which protect children from the rapacity of adults seem to everyone quite as natural as the law against robbery, or the law against polygamy.

In opposition to such an encouraging example, we could cite many facts which show that the moral conscience of the common man has retrogressed badly, in several departments, during the last few generations. The unprecedented scope of the crimes perpetrated by the tyrannies of our time absolutely excludes the optimistic theory which would exonerate the bulk of mankind by referring all the evil to bands of criminals. The bands of criminals who actually directed the movement could not have given it the scope we know that it attained, without the active complicity, at least the tacit consent, the indifference, of countless millions of men. Perfectly capable of sharing in the progress of the moral conscience, these millions of representatives of ordinary humanity demonstrated that the moral conscience of the common man lends itself to every kind of perversion when it no longer finds, in the daily framework of social relations, a discipline which ensures the protection and promotion of moral truths by conferring upon them the effectual reality of familiar impulses. Optimistic and individualistic liberalism has always postulated that moral truth spreads and maintains itself *easily*, by the very force of truth, without the necessity for intervention on the part of the conscious centers of society. This postulate has been refuted by the most striking fact in the history of morals in our time: confusion of conscience in the presence of colossal crimes, amongst ordinary people, decent people, worthy people.

BOOKS BY YVES R. SIMON

1. *Introduction à l'ontologie du connaître.* Paris, 1934. Reprinted 1965 by Brown Reprint Library, Dubuque, Iowa.
2. *Critique de la connaissance morale.* Paris, 1934.
3. *La Campagne d'Ethiopie et la pensée politique Française.* Paris, 1936.
4. *Trois Leçons sur le travail.* Paris, 1938.
5. *Nature and Functions of Authority.* Milwaukee, 1940.
6. *La grande crise de la République Française.* Montreal, 1941. English edition: *The Road to Vichy.* New York, 1942.
7. *La Marche à la délivrance.* New York, 1942. English edition: *The March to Liberation.* Milwaukee, 1942.
8. *Prévoir et savoir.* Montreal, 1944.
9. *Par delà l'expérience du désespoir.* Montreal, 1945. English edition: *Community of the Free.* New York, 1947.
10. *Philosophy of Democratic Government.* Chicago, 1951. Phoenix Books paperback edition, Chicago, 1961.
11. *Traité du libre arbitre.* Liège, 1951.
12. *A General Theory of Authority.* Notre Dame, 1962.
13. *The Tradition of Natural Law.* New York, 1965. Edited by Vukan Kuic.

Index